IN THE SPOTLIGHT

IN THE SPOTLIGHT

*A Guide to Showing Pedigreed
and Household Pet Cats*

By
Carolyn M. Vella
and
John J. McGonagle, Jr.

HOWELL
BOOK HOUSE
New York

Howell Book House
Macmillan Publishing Company
866 Third Avenue, New York, NY 10022
Collier Macmillan Canada, Inc.

Library of Congress Cataloging-in-Publication Data
Vella, Carolyn M.
    In the spotlight : a guide to showing pedigreed and household pet
cats / by Carolyn M. Vella and John J. McGonagle, Jr.
        p.   cm.
    ISBN 0-87605-838-1
    1. Cats—Showing.   I. McGonagle, John J.   II. Title.
SF445.V38   1990
636.8′088′8—dc20   89-29779
                                                                                      CIP

Macmillan books are available at special discounts for bulk purchases for sales promotions, premiums, fund-raising, or educational use. For details contact:

                              Special Sales Director
                              Macmillan Publishing Company
                              866 Third Avenue
                              New York, NY 10022

10 9 8 7 6 5 4 3 2 1

Printed in the United States of America

For Rosaline Dolak De Dan, Ardee Cattery; Jim Becknell, TICA All-Breed Judge; El-Nor's Caligula the Valar (Sascha), our Doberman Pinscher; Pansy, our first cat; and, most of all, for Marge and Ed Golbreski—you are the best friends anyone could ever have.

Contents

About the Authors

Carolyn Vella and **John McGonagle** own a business and two catteries, Jacat and Heart-Nuzzler. They or their catteries are current, active members of the four national federations: American Cat Fanciers Association (ACFA), Cat Fanciers' Association (CFA), Cat Fanciers' Federation (CFF), and The International Cat Association (TICA). Their breed club affiliations include the Happy Household Pet Cat Club (HHPCC) and the Japanese Bobtail Breeders' Society.

Both authors are Certified Head Ring Clerks in TICA. Carolyn Vella has been the vice-president of a cat club and entry clerk for a major cat show. John McGonagle has prepared judges' books and catalogs for cat shows.

They have shown their cats, both pedigreed and household pets, to championship and higher awards in shows sponsored by each of the major national federations.

Acknowledgments

THE AUTHORS would like to thank D. Kent Wallace for his original caricatures, which are used throughout this book. Kent has taught art for twenty-one years. His work has been published in *OMNI* magazine. He is in the Judging Program in ACFA and is a licensed Household Pet judge for that federation.

The authors would also like to thank the following groups and publications for granting them the right to reprint their photographs, materials, forms and logos throughout this book:

American Cat Fanciers Association, Inc. (ACFA).
Cat Fanciers' Federation (CFF).
Cats Magazine, Inc.
Fancy Publications, Inc. (*Cat Fancy*).
Grass Roots Publishing Company, Inc. (*I Love Cats*).
Heinz Pet Products Co. (Morris 9-Lives Materials).
Morris Animal Foundation.
Richard and Daphne Negus (*Cat World™ International*).
The Cat Fanciers' Association, Inc. (CFA).
The International Cat Association (TICA).

Introduction

T HE WORLD of exhibiting pedigreed and Household Pet cats, kittens and Alters has been compared to a circus. People, equipment and animal cages emerge from a variety of vans and cars, enter a vacant area and transform it into a showhall. Empty cages are decorated and then filled with even more decorative cats. People comforts are set up. Cats are fed, watered, and then bathroomed. All of this occurs before 7:00 A.M. on almost every Saturday and Sunday all over the world. It is tiring, beautiful, boring, busy, exhausting, rewarding, frustrating and one of the most exciting things one might do.

This book will explain cat federations and how they relate to showing and titles. We will tell you how to get show information and explain entry procedures for the major national federations. We will discuss show preparations and logistics, including grooming and travel, checking in at the show, setting up your cage and how to manage life in a show hotel. We will take you through the show catalog and tell you who does what at the cat show. Showhall courtesy, an all-important topic, is also covered.

Showing your cat can be a special, exciting experience made even easier if you are as prepared as you can be before the show. Good luck, and we hope to see you at the show!

1

The Cat Federations

THERE ARE SEVERAL cat federations in the United States, as well as separate federations in Canada, Europe and many countries throughout the world. In this country, some federations are national and sanction shows in the majority of states. Other federations currently restrict themselves to certain geographical locations, but may expand in the future.

In general, the federations exist in order to register cats, sanction cat shows and promote the showing and breeding of purebred cats. In addition, cat federations recognize the importance and beauty of household pet cats either through the registration of these cats or by the granting of titles based substantially upon the same point system used to grant titles to purebred cats.

THE NATIONAL FEDERATIONS

This book will concentrate on four major national federations in the United States, based upon the activity of the federation: American Cat Fanciers Association (ACFA), Cat Fanciers' Association (CFA), Cat Fanciers' Federation (CFF), The International Cat Association (TICA). All four major federations have their own systems for scoring cats in order for the cats being shown to achieve titles in that federation. All have some method, either directly or through membership in a cat club, of getting input from members of the federation. They all give some kind

17

of year-end recognition, both nationally and regionally, for cats that scored the highest number of points among all cats competing in that federation's shows during the year. The "show year" for all federations runs from May 1 to April 30. Each federation also has ways of recognizing cats that have produced kittens that have achieved the title of Grand Champion. The federations all communicate through periodic newsletters or through monthly magazines. Each federation also publishes a yearbook after awards are tallied. This yearbook typically carries pictures of the winners along with the federation's activities during the past show year. The yearbook also includes advertisements from breeders and is available to the public as well as to federation members.

Aside from these activities every federation varies somewhat from the others. The emphasis of one may be on a particular aspect of cat breeding or exhibiting. Another may focus on the availability of cat shows in its area or on sponsorship of cat shows around the world. Some emphasize member participation in the federation's activities. Each federation was formed for a specific reason, often dealing with what the founding members felt was a problem with another federation.

Each federation develops a written Standard of Perfection for each of the breeds it recognizes and registers for competition. The standard is formulated through a "breed council." The breed council is made up of those federation members who are active in the breeding and exhibiting of that particular breed of cat. This is the reason you will see some small differences in the cats that are winning in each of the federations. For example, size may be an important factor to the Maine Coon cat in one federation, while another federation does not emphasize size in that breed.

In addition, each federation formulates its own set of rules governing all activities, including:

- How litters are to be registered.
- How individual cats are registered.
- The clerking program and activities of clerks.
- The judging program and activities of judges.
- All aspects of shows, including the scoring of cats.
- The activities of exhibitors.
- How the federation is to be governed.
- All other activities of the federation.

A copy of the show rules is available for a nominal fee from each federation's office. If you are going to show in a particular federation, you should obtain a copy of the current show rules and read them before you attend the show. However, since the rules are constantly being changed and adapted, you will find that not all of the rules are followed to the letter. This can cause some minor problems for the new exhibitor.

If you have a question about the rules, call the federation office. The head office may not know that a rule is being violated. You may also find that a rule has been changed, but the new codified show rules have not yet been printed.

The cat federations all have a genuine interest in the welfare of cats, the perfection of breeds and the recognition of new breeds. However, no matter how well-intentioned, a federation is still a bureaucracy and can have the usual bureaucratic problems. Some federations are slow to return paperwork to you, and some are a bit sporadic with their publications. It is a good idea to keep a copy of any paperwork you send for processing. It may help to enclose a stamped, self-addressed envelope, although this is not really necessary. Always type or print clearly on any form you are filing, and always recheck everything when forms are returned. Mistakes can be made, and they must be corrected.

Most exhibitors tend to choose a federation because of what they perceive as the friendliness of the people who exhibit regularly. However, due to the increasingly high cost of showing cats, many people are no longer exhibiting within just one federation, but are limiting themselves by the geographical location of the shows. The biggest single expense of a cat show is often the cost of the overnight accommodations. If you limit yourself to showing in an area that enables you to come back to your home for the night, you can afford to exhibit at more shows.

For this reason, you will see more and more cats that have titles in two, three or even four federations. This can be an asset for those selling kittens because it shows that your cats are so good that they meet the standard in more than one federation. It is even better for those people buying kittens because the new owner can exhibit the kitten in any of the federations.

If you are interested in becoming a member of any federation, or have questions about activities, contact that federation directly. Each federation generally advertises in one of the magazines devoted to cats, such as *Cats* magazine or *Cat Fancy*. In addition, the cat magazines generally print the names and addresses of all the federations in an annual issue of the magazine. Since not all the federations and other groups have permanent addresses, the annual issue will have the most current address for you to use when you contact a federation.

The Cat Fanciers' Association (CFA) logo.
© 1989.

The American Cat Fanciers Association
(ACFA) logo.   © 1989.

CFF   CAT FANCIERS' FEDERATION, INC.

The Cat Fanciers' Federation (CFF) logo.   © 1989.

The International Cat Association (TICA) logo.   © 1989.

ACFA

ACFA was formed in 1955 by a group of cat Fanciers seeking greater flexibility in the development of cats. They also sought expanded activities for cat lovers and greater growth and harmony with contemporary needs of breeders and the cat Fancy at large. This federation was the first to promote multiple titles and the first to recognize wins from other "recognized" associations that could apply to multiple championship titles. It was also the first to judge the altered cat in championship competition in a separate class. ACFA also began the practice of the multiple-ring championship show. The federation is active in the United States, Canada, Europe, Australia and Japan, and had the first American judge to officiate behind the Iron Curtain, at a show in Budapest, Hungary.

The American Cat Fanciers Association, Inc.
P.O. Box 203
Point Lookout, MO 65726

CFA

CFA was founded in 1906 to provide registry services to the owners, breeders and exhibitors of purebred cats, and in 1987 processed its one-millionth cat registration. In 1988 alone, it registered seventy-five thousand cats. In addition, CFA provides services such as genetic screening of applications to assure the integrity of pedigrees, cattery reports to help breeders stay informed regarding the achievements of cats of their breeding and recognition programs for both breeders and owners. It also publishes a variety of pamphlets and a monthly magazine. The federation is active in the United States, Canada, Japan and France. In 1968, CFA established the Robert H. Winn Foundation, which encourages the study of feline health and provides funds to the various schools of veterinary medicine throughout the United States. CFA underwrites the operating expenses of the foundation so that 100 percent of its donations are used for grants.

The Cat Fanciers' Association, Inc.
1309 Allaire Avenue
Ocean, NJ 07712

CFF

CFF was chartered in 1919 in Connecticut. The executive board, which governs the organization, is elected through a system of one vote per club. In 1988, CFF set a milestone by being the first federation to offer yearly award recognition to both Experimental and Any Other Variety (AOV) breeds. These are breeds of cats not currently recognized for Championship competition. CFF has clubs in the United States and Canada, along with affiliates in Norway and Sweden. In 1973, the All Points Cat Club was started, offering membership across the country to people in areas with no current CFF clubs. Because of this national club, additional interest in CFF has been generated, with new clubs being formed and shows being held in areas where there had not been any prior CFF activity.

> Cat Fanciers' Federation, Inc. (CFF)
> Office of the Recorder
> 9509 Montgomery Road
> Cincinnati, OH 45242

TICA

TICA was organized in the summer of 1979 to sponsor and promote the welfare of all cats, including Household Pets. TICA promotes and encourages kindness to all animals and assists in the prevention of cruelty and mistreatment of animals, in part by encouraging the spaying and neutering of any and all cats not specifically being used as part of a viable breeding program. Additionally, it carries on the usual registration and cat show licensing activities. In TICA, Household Pets earn titles directly equivalent to those of the purebred, breeding-quality cats. TICA is active in the United States, Canada, Japan, Europe and South America. A toll-free 800 number provides show information to exhibitors in the United States and Canada. That number is: 1-800-TICA-INF in the United States, and 1-800-344-TICA in Canada.

> The International Cat Association, Inc. (TICA)
> P.O Box 2684
> Harlingen, TX 78551

REGIONAL AND LOCAL FEDERATIONS

In addition to the four major national cat federations, there are other federations active in promoting cat shows. These may be limited to a particular geographical location and may be the most convenient when you show your cats. Examples of the regional federations are The American Cat Association, The United Cat Federation and The Canadian Cat Association.

Pet Pride of New York, Inc., was represented at a CFF show in Albany, New York. Most cat clubs encourage cat-related charities by providing space for them at the shows. Purebred cat exhibitors and breeders never lose sight of the continuing need for protection of all cats. Pet Pride provides shelter, neutering and health care for the cats in their care, and a comprehensive adoption service for cats.

Cat shows always find a place for an animal-related charity.

If you find a show that is being sponsored by one of the regional federations, and you are interested in attending that show or even joining the federation, contact the show's Entry Clerk. The Entry Clerk will be able to give you the current address of the home office. You can contact this office for the current rules and breed standards in which you are interested.

CAT CLUBS

A cat club is a group of people who get together to put on cat shows. Most cat clubs are affiliated with one of the cat federations, so that the wins of the cats at the show can be scored for titles and for regional and national points. For example, the Garden State Cat Club of New Jersey is affiliated with CFA, and the Conestoga Cat Club is affiliated with ACFA. If you exhibit your cat at the Garden State Cat Club show, your points will be scored and kept by CFA, but if you exhibit the same cat at the Conestoga show, you will be gaining points in ACFA.

Sanctioned Shows

Each show is "sanctioned" by the club's parent federation. This means that the club has gotten approval to hold the show from the federation. In return, the club agrees that the show will be run under that federation's rules, and that it will scored according to the system used by that federation. The breed Standards applied are those accepted by that federation, and the judges are licensed by that federation.

Nonsanctioned Shows

If you exhibit at a show that is labeled "nonsanctioned," you cannot gain points in any federation. A nonsanctioned show is usually held to promote the care of cats, usually nonpedigreed, and is governed only by any rules adopted by a committee putting on the show. If the sponsoring committee is a local humane society, you may find the show is unlike any other you have seen. For example, you may be required to keep your cat in a travel cage instead of a benching cage. Or the judges may have no direct connection with the breeding or exhibiting of purebred cats. Sometimes, you will find a nonsanctioned show is being put on by a club that is affiliated with a federation. Such shows are generally run in the same way as a sanctioned cat show, with minor variations. For example, the judges handling the cats may or may not have completed a full training program sponsored by the federation and, therefore, may not be licensed judges. But the most important difference for exhibitors is that no points or honors earned at that show will be used in scoring for titles, or in regional or national wins.

Show Details

Even though several cat clubs may be affiliated with the same federation, their shows may not be the same. Clubs have quite a bit of leeway in how a show is actually run. The club can control the size of the show by limiting the number of cats that can be entered. It can decide whether it will permit a Household Pet ring at all and whether the Household Pet cats have to be declawed in order to be shown.

Because the clubs can decide on many aspects of the show, they eventually get reputations for the quality of shows they produce. Some clubs try to save money by buying small Finals rosettes, while other clubs not only present big, beautiful rosettes, but also present trophies and prizes. Some clubs have their shows at first-class hotels, while others will use a school gymnasium as a showhall.

The club show committee will also choose the judges who will be judging at the show. Judges are chosen for many different reasons, not the least of which is how far away the judge lives from the show. The club has to pay the judges' expenses. These can be considerable if all judges have flown in from a distance.

In general, as long as the show is well managed, it will be enjoyable. Every club will do its best to put on a well-managed show.

The Meaning of Titles

The purpose of breeding cats is not just to have kittens, but rather to produce top-quality show cats. Every thought-out breeding program has this as its aim. If you talk to breeders of quality cats, you will find that they have a great knowledge of genetics. If you are allowed into their cattery, look at all the genetics books on the shelf. The application of those genetic principles may vary from breeder to breeder, but that is a matter of experience and personal choice.

Titled Pedigreed Cats

In order to obtain the stud services of a top-quality male cat, buy a show-quality kitten or just validate a breeding program, breeders will show their best cats. *The titles these cats earn are important to the breeder and to the cattery because they recognize excellence.* If you look at the breeder's advertisements in cat magazines, you will see ads that state what "line" the cats come from. A well-regarded line is the highlight of a breeder's career.

Breeders who produce only pet-quality kittens are not highly regarded in the cat Fancy. Of course, you can breed two show-quality cats and get a litter that is all pet quality. This will eventually happen to everyone. Breeding is, after all, not an exact science. However, some breeders just breed cats in order to sell kittens. Their kittens are usually priced at the high end of the pet-quality price range, and they don't always check out the new owners thoroughly. They also don't care to keep up with the cats after they are sold. Unfortunately, breeders sometimes sell a cat who is sick. When this happens, the new owner may be heartbroken and may stay away from purchasing a purebred cat in the future.

Titled Household Pets

Once, at a show, a spectator asked why someone would spend so much time and money to get a title on an HHP (Household Pet). The answer given was, "ego." In our opinion, this is not true and is an insult to the Household Pet exhibitor. There are many reasons why HHPs are shown. The most common reason is that the cat is truly adored. Exhibitors want other people to appreciate the beauty of their "alley cat" or of their pet-quality purebred cat. A title confirms that judges are as appreciative of the cat as you are.

We learned how to show cats by showing our HHPs. It takes a long time to decide upon a specific breed and many factors go into that decision. Going to shows helps you get to know all the breeds and talk to various breeders. When we had decided on our breed, we started our search for a foundation queen for our cattery. One of the things that encouraged breeders to sell us a show-quality cat was that we had exhibited our HHPs to the title of Supreme Grand Master. In other words, we knew what we were doing because we had been through it.

Some people rescue cats in distress. They clean them up, take care of them until they are in peak health, neuter them, socialize them and begin to show them. After the cats are used to people and trust them, the exhibitor may then try to place these cats in loving homes—giving up all the rosettes and titles they have worked so hard to help the cat earn. People who do this are totally unselfish. They live through the heartbreak of seeing cats who have been abused or abandoned. They suffer through the deliveries of kittens by a mother cat who may be half-

A cat show is a good place to purchase a kitten.

Sassy slept on the arm of the sofa even before she became a Supreme Grand Master.

starved and sick. They lose cats to death no matter how hard they try to save them. These people do this because of their love for all cats. When they have pulled a cat through all this, they don't show these cats to gratify their egos. These people are to be admired.

When some judges award their Finals in the HHP ring, they have exhibitors talk a little bit about their cat. If you ever get a chance to listen to this, by all means do so. It is hard to listen if you love cats. It is even harder if you are one of those who has to talk about the cat. You will hear stories about how cats were rescued from harrowing experiences, or found abandoned. You will hear how various cats got their names. You will also hear a lot about the cats themselves, the things that make them special. This, in its own way, is the most important Final at any show.

2

Registering Your Cat

$\mathbf{A}$ CAT THAT is "registered" has a special cachet. For the purebred cat, whether show quality or pet quality, registration means that the litter was born to purebred parents. For the HHP, it shows the cat is so special that you wanted it to be recognized as such.

When you buy a purebred cat from breeders, they will give you the paperwork necessary for the cat to be registered with the various federations. If your breeder is reluctant to permit you to register a pet-quality cat with a purebred registry, you still have an opportunity to register the cat by registering the cat as a Household Pet. You don't need the breeder's permission to do this. In some federations, the cat can carry the cattery designation if you so desire (and this has not been specifically prohibited in your sales agreement). In other federations, you must have the breeder's signature if the cattery designation is to be used. If you have adopted a special cat, but you don't know who the parents are, register the cat as a HHP.

HOW TO READ A REGISTERED NAME

The name of a purebred cat looks intimidating until you break it down into its elements. For example, "GRC Nekomo Caught in the Act of Jacat" is read this way:

- *GRC:* This means the cat is a Grand Champion in one of the federations that grants the title.

CFF

CAT FANCIERS' FEDERATION, INC.
9509 MONTGOMERY ROAD
CINCINNATI, OHIO-45242
513/984-1841

A CFF cattery registration form.
© 1989.

CFF CATTERY REGISTRATION FORM/PLEASE PRINT OR TYPE

I HEREBY APPLY FOR THE FOLLOWING CFF REGISTERED CATTERY NAME:

FIRST CHOICE_____

SECOND CHOICE_____
FEE OF $25.00 IS ENCLOSED.

OWNER(S) NAME_____

ADDRESS_____

_____

_____

SIGNED_____

DATE_____

**USE OF A REGISTERED CATTERY NAME IS RESTRICTED TO THE REGISTERED OWNER(S).

****
(For Office Use Only)

Cattery Name_____

Cattery Registration Number_____

Date_____.

CFF

A CFF certificate of registration of cattery name.   © 1989.

CERTIFICATE OF REGISTRATION
OF CATTERY NAME

Cat Fanciers' Federation

This Certifies that the Name _____ H-N _____ #6414 _____
has been registered under the Rules of the Cat Fanciers' Federation as a Cattery Name

by Carolyn M. Vella-John J. McGonagle _____

for Their exclusive use in registering pedigrees in this Federation.

Date ___3/31/88___   Signed _____

Fee $25.00   Recorder of Registrations

An ACFA cattery registration form.   © 1989.

ACFA

| BREEDER'S ACFA CATTERY NAME AND NUMBER | LITTER REG. NUMBER | |

FIRST NAME CHOICE

SECOND NAME CHOICE

OWNER'S NAME(S)

ADDRESS _____   BREEDER

ADDRESS _____   OWNER

CITY _____ STATE _____ ZIP _____   SIRE

OWNER(S) CATTERY NAME _____ NUMBER _____   DAM

— TO BE COMPLETED BY BREEDER —

COLOR: _____   BREED   BIRTHDATE

SEX: _____ EYE COLOR: _____

BREEDER'S SIGNATURE(S):   IF CHECKED, ☐ NOT TO BE USED FOR BREEDING -or- ☐ TO BE RECORDED AS A HHP
SIGNATURE REQUIRED X _____   DATE: _____

A CFF litter registration form. © 1989.

LITTER REGISTRATION
CAT FANCIERS' FEDERATION

SECTION A
- Breed
- Date of Birth
- Number of Living Males
- Number of Living Females

SECTION B
- Owner of Sire at Time of Mating
- Complete Address
- Signature
- Owner of Dam at Time of Mating
- Complete Address
- Signature
- Breeder's CFF Cattery Name _____

SECTION C

1.
- Name of Sire
- Color
- Registration Number

2.
- Name of Dam
- Color
- Registration Number

IF ALL INFORMATION INCLUDING CFF REG. NO IS SHOWN ON CATS 1 & 2 NO FURTHER PEDIGREE NEED BE GIVEN

3.
- Sire of Sire
- Registration Number
- Dam of Sire
- Registration Number

4.
- Sire of Dam
- Registration Number
- Dam of Dam
- Registration Number

TICA — LITTER REGISTRATION APPLICATION

MAIL APPLICATION WITH FEE TO

THE INTERNATIONAL CAT ASSOCIATION
P.O. BOX 2684
HARLINGEN, TEXAS 78551

(Please read instructions on reverse side before completing application)

TYPE OR PRINT   SECTION A

BREED	DATE OF BIRTH	NO. OF LIVING FEMALES MALES

SECTION B — SIRE

- BREED / REGISTERED NAME OF SIRE
- REGISTRATION NUMBER / COLOR
- OWNER OF SIRE AT TIME OF MATING
- STREET ADDRESS
- CITY / STATE / ZIP
- SIGNATURE / CATTERY NAME (IF ANY)

SECTION C — DAM

- BREED / REGISTERED NAME OF DAM
- REGISTRATION NUMBER / COLOR
- OWNER OF DAM AT TIME OF MATING (OR LEASEE)
- STREET ADDRESS
- CITY / STATE / ZIP
- SIGNATURE / CATTERY NAME (IF ANY)

I hereby certify that the above statement is ture and correct.

SECTION D (Complete this section ONLY to register individual kittens) | **SECTION E** (Enter 2 choices of name and name and address of owner)

1
- SEX
- COLOR
- EYE COLOR
- LH☐ SH☐
- CE☐ SE☐

- NAME (1ST CHOICE)
- NAME (2ND CHOICE)
- OWNER
- STREET ADDRESS
- CITY / STATE / ZIP

A TICA litter registration application form. © 1989.

An ACFA litter registration form. © 1989.

INSTRUCTIONS

LITTER REGISTRATION

GENERAL REGISTRATION RULES: ALL LITTER APPLICATIONS MUST COMPLETE THE FOLLOWING
- Number of Males and Females
- Breed
- Birthdate
- Sex and Color of each kitten
- Signatures of the Breeder, Owner of Litter, and the Owner of the Sire
- Address of the Owner of the Litter
- Breeder's cattery name and number; if the cattery is not registered with ACFA denote "Not Applicable".
- **SIRE & DAM BLOCKS:** Complete their full registered names, ACFA registration number if registered with ACFA, breed, color & pattern, eye color, and birthdate.

SIRE AND/OR DAM NOT REGISTERED WITH ACFA
- A photographic copy of the registration certificate from the association with which the cat is registered must accompany the litter registration application.
  SIRE: Must complete blocks 3, 4, 7, 8, 9, and 10. Be sure to list the full registration number as well as the initials of the association with which the cats are registered.
- **DAM:** Must complete blocks 5, 6, 11, 12, 13, and 14. Be sure to list the full registration number as well as the initials of the association with which the cats are registered.

LITTER REGISTRATION FEES EFFECTIVE JANUARY 1, 1988
- DAM & SIRE REGISTERED WITH ACFA....................$5.00
- DAM AND/OR SIRE NOT REGISTERED WITH ACFA..........$10.00
- REGISTRATION OF A KITTEN $6.00

REGISTRATION OF KITTEN AT TIME OF LITTER REGISTRATION

SERIAL #	NAME CHOICE (May not exceed 35 letters & spaces)	OWNER'S NAME and ADDRESS

PLEASE ALLOW 15 DAYS FOR PROCESSING

MAIL TO AMERICAN CAT FANCIERS ASSOCIATION PH: 417-334-5430
PO BOX 537
PT LOOKOUT, MO. 65726

31

THE CAT FANCIERS' ASSOCIATION, INC. LITTER APPLICATION

Please read instructions on reverse side before completing application.

#2062-12/87

Please Type or Print   **SECTION A — Birth Information**

Breed	Date of Birth Month/Day/Year	# of Living Females	Males

SECTION B — Sire Information

Registered Name of Sire

CFA Registration Number   Signature of Sire's Owner/Lessee

Owner/Lessee of Sire at Time of Mating

Address

City   State/Province   Zip/Postal Code

SECTION C — Breeder & Dam Information

Registered Name of Dam

CFA Registration Number   Color

Name of Breeder of Litter

Breeder's Address

City   State/Province   Zip/Postal Code

Breeder's CFA Registered Cattery Name (if any)   Breeder #/ Cattery #   Signature of Breeder of Litter

Please check ☐ This is my first litter registration with CFA.
if applicable. ☐ I have recently moved. My previous zip code was _____

OPTIONAL   SECTION D — Lease

On the date of mating, this dam was leased to the person listed in Section C.

Signature of the Registered Owner of the Dam on the Date of Mating.   Breeder #   Date

OPTIONAL   SECTION E — Litter Owner
(Complete only if owner different from breeder.)

Name of Owner

Owner's Address

City   State/Province   Zip/Postal Code

Owner's Cattery Number   Signature of Owner of Litter

SECTION F — Kitten Registrations   (Complete this section ONLY to register individual kittens)
(Enter 2 choices of name, and name and address of owner)

Name of Cat (1st Choice)

Name of Cat (2nd Choice)

Sex   Color   Eye Color   Office Use Only

Owner Name

Address

City   State/Province   Zip/Postal Code

A CFA litter registration form.   © 1989.

The Cat Fanciers' Association, Inc.

CERTIFICATE OF REGISTRATION-LITTER

BREED: PERSIAN   LITTER NO. 439845   BREEDER: JUDY-GREG B

DATE OF BIRTH: 07/22/86   BR. NO. 010363

SIRE: GC SOUTH PAW MOONLIGHTING   102-291836 V0886

DAM: GC JOVAN MOVIE STAR OF SOUTH PAW   115-233333 V0586

MALES: 2

JUDY-GREG B   FEMALES: 2

OWNER
ROME   GA   30161   DATE: 05/22/89

A CFA certificate of registered litter.   © 1989.

32

American Cat Fanciers Association, Inc.

P.O. Box 203
Point Lookout, Missouri 65726

Date Reg.	Date Re-Reg.	Reason for Re-Reg.	Registration Number

Provide three choices of names.
[Please print or type]

1. _____

2. _____

3. _____

Reg.No._____

Assoc._____

Breed_____

Color_____ Eye Color_____

Sex_____ Date of Birth_____

_____
Owner of Cat to be Registered

_____
Street Address

_____
City/State/Zip Code

_____
Owner's Cattery Name and ACFA No.

_____
Breeder's Cattery Name and ACFA No.

Breeder's signature: Required If Dam is ACFA Registered.

Application Fee – $12.00

1. Sire:_____

Reg.No._____

Breed_____

Color_____

Eye Color_____ Birth Date_____

NOTE: If Sire and/or Dam are not registered in ACFA then the ancestry in Blocks #3, 4, 7-10 and/or 5, 6, 11-14 must be completed.

2. Dam:_____

Reg.No._____

Breed_____

Color_____

Eye Color_____ Birth Date_____

PROOF OF REGISTRATION: If the cat to be registered is registered with another Association, a 'zerox' copy of its registration certificate must be submitted with the application. If the cat is not registered then proof of registration will be submitted for the Dam and/or Sire if not registered with ACFA.

3. Sire_____

Reg.No._____ Breed & Color_____

4. Dam_____

Reg.No._____ Breed & Color_____

5. Sire_____

Reg.No._____ Breed & Color_____

6. Dam_____

Reg.No._____ Breed & Color_____

7. Sire_____

Reg.No._____ Breed/Color_____

8. Dam_____

Reg.No._____ Breed/Color_____

9. Sire_____

Reg.No._____ Breed/Color_____

10. Dam_____

Reg.No._____ Breed/Color_____

11. Sire_____

Reg.No._____ Breed/Color_____

12. Dam_____

Reg.No._____ Breed/Color_____

13. Sire_____

Reg.No._____ Breed/Color_____

14. Dam_____

Reg.No._____ Breed/Color_____

APPLICATION FOR REGISTRATION OF CAT NOT LITTER REGISTERED WITH ACFA

An ACFA application form to register a cat. © 1989.

TICA

P.O. BOX 2988, HARLINGEN, TX 78551

APPLICATION FOR REGISTRATION

Name of Cat _____

Born _____ Breed _____

Reg. Nu. _____ Color _____

Eye Color _____ Sex _____

Owner _____

Address _____

Cattery Name _____ Tica No. _____

PARENTS	GRANDPARENTS	GREAT GRANDPARENTS

SIRE _____

Reg. No. _____ Breed _____

Color _____ Sex _____ Eye Color _____

Owner _____

Address _____

Cattery Name _____ Tica No. _____

Signature of Owner _____

DAM _____

Reg. No. _____ Breed _____

Color _____ Sex _____ Eye Color _____

Owner _____

Address _____

Cattery Name _____ Tica No. _____

Signature of Owner _____

(GRANDPARENTS)
No. _____ Breed/Color _____
No. _____ Breed/Color _____
No. _____ Breed/Color _____
No. _____ Breed/Color _____

(GREAT GRANDPARENTS)
No. _____ Breed/Color _____
Nu. _____ Breed/Color _____
No. _____ Breed/Color _____
No. _____ Breed/Color _____
No. _____ Breed/Color _____
No. _____ Breed/Color _____
No. _____ Breed/Color _____
No. _____ Breed/Color _____

I certify that to the best of my knowledge and belief, the above pedigree is true and correct.

Signed _____ Date _____

A TICA application form to register a cat. © 1989.

33

- *Nekomo:* This is the registered cattery name of the cattery that bred the cat.
- *Caught in the Act:* This is the cat's registered name.
- *Of Jacat:* This means it is owned by a cattery with the registered name "Jacat."

GENERAL RULES FOR REGISTRATION

Whether you are registering a purebred cat or an HHP, some general suggestions apply:

- Enclose all appropriate paperwork and the required fee.
- Type the form, or print clearly. Otherwise a mistake can be made.
- Include photocopies of any original forms, such as the breeder's pedigree or the neutering certificate. Do not include originals.
- Keep a copy of the registration form as you filled it out.
- If you have any questions, contact the federation directly.
- Allow enough time for the paperwork to be completed before you check on the status of the registration.
- Sometimes you will have a question about how a particular cat should be registered within the breed. If so, enclose a picture of the cat along with the registration form. For example, every federation has a different way of describing color classes. If the federation has a picture to go by, it will have no difficulty classifying a cat.

THE PEDIGREE FORM

The pedigree is the family tree for your cat. Many pedigree certificate forms may be used when a cat is sold with its pedigree. Some are designed by the breeder, some are provided to the breeder by various cat food manufacturers, and some are form pedigrees you can buy or generate on your computer. The pedigree lists ancestors, their titles and sometimes their registration numbers, along with other pertinent information, such as the color of the cats in the line.

THE LITTER REGISTRATION

Unless you are a breeder, you will not have to register a litter of kittens. When a purebred litter is born, the litter itself is registered with

CFA INC. CAT REGISTRATION APPLICATION

INSTRUCTIONS: LIMIT NAME TO 35 SPACES-BREEDER'S CFA REGISTERED CATTERY NAME PREFIX (IF ANY) MUST BE INCLUDED.

BREEDER'S CFA REGISTERED CATTERY NAME

PRINT ONE
LETTER
PER BOX
– SKIP A
BOX BETWEEN
WORDS –
PUNCTUATION
IN ITS
OWN BOX

CAT'S NAME

1st CHOICE

2nd CHOICE

ISSUE DATE:

BREED:

DATE OF BIRTH:

SIRE:

DAM: sample – SAMPLE

LITTER NO.:

BR./CATTERY NO:

BREEDER:

OWNER(s) NAME(s)

STREET

CITY

STATE/PROVINCE

ZIP/POSTAL CODE

THIS AREA MUST BE COMPLETED BY BREEDER

COLOR OF CAT:
(SEE REVERSE)

COAT LENGTH:
(CIRCLE ONE) Long Short

SEX:

EYE COLOR:

DATE of SALE:

MONTH DAY YEAR

☐ THIS CAT MAY NOT BE USED FOR BREEDING. (IF CHECKED, SIGNATURE OF NEW OWNER REQUIRED; UNSIGNED APPLICATIONS WILL BE RETURNED.)

CFA INC. RESERVES THE RIGHT TO CORRECT OR REVOKE FOR CAUSE ANY REGISTRATION CERTIFICATE ISSUED. ANY ERASURE AND/OR ALTERATION MAY VOID THIS CERTIFICATE.

A CFA (blue slip) cat registration form. © *1989.*

TICA

HOUSEHOLD PET REGISTRATION APPLICATION

Please type or print all information.
FEE: $5.00

Date_____

CAT'S NAME _____ BIRTHDATE_____ LH_____SH_____

NEUTER_____SPAY_____

DATE ALTERED_____

COLOR & PATTERN _____ EYE COLOR _____

SIRE (if known)_____ DAM (if known)_____

OWNER'S NAME_____ ST. ADDRESS_____

CITY _____ STATE_____ ZIP_____PHONE _____

NOTICE

TITLES are confirmed ONLY on altered Household Pets.

MAIL TO: **THE INTERNATIONAL CAT ASSOCIATION**
P.O. BOX 2684, HARLINGEN, TX 78551

A TICA form to register a Household Pet. © *1989.*

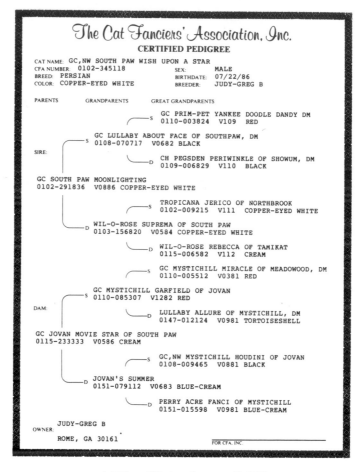

The Cat Fanciers' Association, Inc.
CERTIFICATE OF REGISTRATION

NAME OF CAT: GC,NW SOUTH PAW WISH UPON A STAR   0102-345118
CFA Registration #

DESCRIPTION: COPPER-EYED WHITE PERSIAN MALE BORN 07/22/86

SIRE: GC SOUTH PAW MOONLIGHTING   0102-291836 V0886
CFA Registration #

DAM: GC JOVAN MOVIE STAR OF SOUTH PAW   0115-233333 V0586
CFA Registration #

OWNER: JUDY-GREG B   BREEDER: JUDY-GREG B
ROME, GA 30161

DATE: 05/22/89   439845

A CFA certificate of registration.   © 1989.

The Cat Fanciers' Association, Inc.
CERTIFIED PEDIGREE

CAT NAME: GC,NW SOUTH PAW WISH UPON A STAR
CFA NUMBER: 0102-345118   SEX: MALE
BREED: PERSIAN   BIRTHDATE: 07/22/86
COLOR: COPPER-EYED WHITE   BREEDER: JUDY-GREG B

PARENTS   GRANDPARENTS   GREAT GRANDPARENTS

SIRE:

GC SOUTH PAW MOONLIGHTING
0102-291836 V0886 COPPER-EYED WHITE

S   GC LULLABY ABOUT FACE OF SOUTHPAW, DM
    0108-070717 V0682 BLACK

S   GC PRIM-PET YANKEE DOODLE DANDY DM
    0110-003824 V109 RED

D   CH PEGSDEN PERIWINKLE OF SHOWUM, DM
    0109-006829 V110 BLACK

D   WIL-O-ROSE SUPREMA OF SOUTH PAW
    0103-156820 V0584 COPPER-EYED WHITE

S   TROPICANA JERICO OF NORTHBROOK
    0102-009215 V111 COPPER-EYED WHITE

D   WIL-O-ROSE REBECCA OF TAMIKAT
    0115-006582 V112 CREAM

DAM:

GC JOVAN MOVIE STAR OF SOUTH PAW
0115-233333 V0586 CREAM

S   GC MYSTICHILL GARFIELD OF JOVAN
    0110-085307 V1282 RED

S   GC MYSTICHILL MIRACLE OF MEADOWOOD, DM
    0110-005512 V0381 RED

D   LULLABY ALLURE OF MYSTICHILL, DM
    0147-012124 V0981 TORTOISESHELL

D   JOVAN'S SUMMER
    0151-079112 V0683 BLUE-CREAM

S   GC,NW MYSTICHILL HOUDINI OF JOVAN
    0108-009465 V0881 BLACK

D   PERRY ACRE FANCI OF MYSTICHILL
    0151-015598 V0981 BLUE-CREAM

OWNER: JUDY-GREG B
ROME, GA 30161

FOR CFA, INC.

A CFA certified pedigree.   © 1989.

the various cat federations. This enables the kittens from that litter to be registered as individual cats. A proof of pedigree is required, and a fee is charged.

REGISTERING AN INDIVIDUAL CAT

When you buy a purebred cat you intend to register with one of the federations, the breeder should provide you with all the information that is necessary to register the cat. Obtain a registration form from the federation or federations with which you want the cat registered and follow all the instructions carefully. Print or type the application clearly, enclose the required fee and mail this to the appropriate federation. Most federations limit the number of letters you can use in the name of the cat. Remember that the cattery name of the breeding cattery is part of the name and counts in the letter total, as does your cattery name if you are using one.

You will receive a form from the registering federation that is your cat's official certificate of registration. You will need this when you enter a cat show and when you claim your cat's wins.

Registering Household Pet Cats

Registering an HHP with one of the federations that registers, or records, them is very easy. Fill out the form clearly and completely and enclose the required fee and a copy of the neutering certificate, if that is required.

You will get a certificate from the federation, and you will use this the same way you use a registration certificate for a purebred cat. When you enter a show, use your cat's registration number. Use the number for claiming titles and for all other purposes when dealing with the federation with which you have registered your HHP.

HOW TO READ A CERTIFICATE OF REGISTRATION

A sample certificate of registration is shown on p. 36. It contains the following information:

- *The Cat Fanciers' Association, Inc.:* This is the recording registry.
- *Name of cat:* This is the name the cat will be known by officially. No other cat will ever be allowed to use this name.

American Cat Fanciers Association, Inc.
P.O. Box 203, Point Lookout, Missouri 65726

APPLICATION FOR "RECORDING"
HOUSEHOLD PET..

Name of Cat to be "Recorded" _____ Male __ Female __

Owner's Name: _____

Address: _____
(Street No.   (City)   (State)   (Zip)

Certification: The above named cat was "Surgically Sterilized" (altered) on _____

by: _____   _____
(Name of Vet/Clinic)   (Signature of Vet or Owner)

(NOTE: All "Adult" Household Pets over 8 months old must be altered to be recorded.)

MIXED BREEDS ONLY

Longhair Cat:_____ Shorthair Cat:_____ Date of Birth: _____
        (Check One)   (Approximate years if Unk.)

Color Pattern (Check One): Solid Color (one color) _____ Bi-color (2 colors) _____

        Parti-color (3 or more colors) _____   Tabby (solid color with stripes) _____

Eye Color:_____ Coat Color (describe briefly):_____

_____

PUREBRED ONLY

Breed: _____ Color: _____

Was this cat "Individually" Registered with ACFA?   YES _____   NO _____

Was this cat "Litter" Registered with ACFA?   YES _____   NO _____

Litter Number: L-_____ Registration No. _____
(NOTE: If this Cat has been "Individually" Registered with ACFA, the Certificate of
        Registration must accompany this application, to be surrendered to ACFA....)

Breeder's Name: _____

Breeder's Cattery Name: _____ ACFA No. _____

(NOTE: If Breeder's Cattery name is to be used as a "Prefix" to the Cat's name, the
        Breeder must sign the following authorization.)

As the above named breeder of the Purebred Household Pet to be recorded, I hereby auth-
orize my ACFA Registered Cattery name to be used as a "Prefix" to the Recorded Name...

_____   _____
(Breeder's Signature)   (Date)

Recording Fee: $5.00

HHP-1

An ACFA form to record or register a Household Pet.   © 1989.

CAT FANCIERS' FEDERATION, INC.

HOUSEHOLD PET REGISTRATION FORM-PLEASE TYPE OR PRINT.

CFF

NAME_____

BREED_____ LH_____ SH_____

COLOR_____

DATE OF BIRTH_____ SEX_____ SPAY_____ NEUTER_____

OWNER_____

ADDRESS_____

CITY_____ STATE_____ ZIP_____

SIGNATURE_____

Please include a last name or other distinguishing title to your cat's name since we cannot duplicate names, and this will help to avoid conflict in our records.

***All CFF registered Household Pets are now eligible to be confirmed as a Companion, Grand Companion, and Master Grand Companion. SEE REVERSE SIDE FOR RULES OF COMPETITION.

MAIL APPLICATION AND $5.00 FEE TO: CAT FANCIERS' FEDERATION, INC.
9509 MONTGOMERY RD.
CINCINNATI, OHIO-45242
513/984-1841

CFF RESERVES THE RIGHT TO REVOKE OR RESCIND ANY REGISTRATION ERRONEOUSLY ENROLLED OR IN VIOLATION OF CFF RULES OF REGISTRATION.

A CFF form to register a Household Pet. © 1989.

- *Description:* This is the official description of the cat, including the date of birth.
- *CFA registration number:* This is the number assigned to your cat. You will use this number during the lifetime of your cat for all CFA purposes. This is how they know your cat.
- *Sire:* This is the official name, followed by the registration number, of your cat's father.
- *Dam:* This is the official name, followed by the registration number, of your cat's mother.
- *Owner:* This is the registered owner of the cat at the time of registration.
- *Breeder:* This is the breeder of your cat.
- *Date:* This is the date the cat was registered.

CATTERY REGISTRATION

It is not necessary to have a registered cattery in order to show cats. The following information is provided to show the process of registration.

When you have a cattery, you register the name of the cattery with the various federations where you will be registering your litters and your cats. Each federation has its own form and its own rules. Most federations limit the number of letters you can use in the name of your cattery, and a fee is charged to register (and, in some federations, to maintain registration of) your cattery. The cattery name can be used only by the registered cattery owner and applies only to those cats the cattery breeds or owns.

We have two registered catteries. One is a nonbreeding cattery. Our HHPs are part of this cattery and carry this cattery name as part of their name. The other cattery is a breeding cattery. Our purebred, breeding cats are part of this cattery.

3

Obtaining Show Information

THE EASIEST WAY to get information on future cat shows is through one of the cat magazines that print the show schedule. However, these schedules may not be complete. For a complete list of shows being sponsored by a given federation, contact the federation directly.

The magazines and bulletins published by various federations will carry that federation's show schedule. However, given the lead time for printing, they may not be completely current.

Show information listed by a publication may not answer all your questions. Cat clubs announce shows months in advance and may not have every detail decided. Various magazines use different formats and have a limited amount of space to accommodate show schedules. If you need more information, or have a question, contact the Entry Clerk (EC) with your question.

MAGAZINES

Magazines devoted exclusively to cats aim to be of interest to all cat lovers. They usually include services for the cat show exhibitor. These services range from minimal to extensive, depending on the desires of the magazine staff and the information provided by the show-giving clubs.

The show calendar from *Cat Fancy* magazine.
© 1989 Fancy Publications, Inc.

March 1989

3-5 **New York, New York:** INCATS/Garden CC (TICA). Madison Square Garden. Judges: Brown, Caruthers, Me. Coleman, Harding, Hogan, Pannell, Patrick, Paul, Savant, Scheuermann, Shaw, Stephens, Tullo, Zear. Info: Barry Goldstein, 40 Clinton St., Brooklyn, NY 11201; (718) 855-1928. EBCD: Jan. 23.

4-5 **Bradenton, Florida:** Fiesta CF (ACFA). Info: Gayle Bringman, 423 47th St. N.W., Bradenton, FL 34209; (813) 746-3469.

4-5 **Davenport, Iowa:** Illinois and Iowa CF (ACFA). Judges (Sat.): AB—Alitz, Herbst; LH/SH—Ober-Rodgers, Summers. Judges (Sun.): AB—Boeger, Jordan; LH/SH—Lawrence, Roney. Info: Doris Sandvick, R.R. #1, Box 187, Long Grove, IA 52803; (319) 225-6191.

4-5 **Shreveport, Louisiana:** Pelican State CC (CFA). Shreveport Convention Center, 600 Fannin St. Judges: AB—Bradshaw, Darrah, Owen, J. Thompson, Wheelwright, D. Williams; LH/SH—Fuller, Salisbury. Info: Mary Biedenkapp, 10672 Hannon Rd., Cherry Valley, CA 92223; (714) 845-7598.

4-5 **Boston, Massachusetts:** Cats—Plain and Fancy (CFA). Copley Marriott, 110 Huntington Ave. Judges (Sat.): AB—Barnaby, Trevathan; LH/SH—Mellies. Judges (Sun.): AB—Kachel, D.J. Thompson; LH/SH—Hutzler. Info: Lee Imes, P.O. Box 17361, Rochester, NY 14617; (716) 436-8141 or (617) 262-5639.

4-5 **Cortland, New York:** Fantastic Felines of CNY (CFA). Holiday Inn. Judges: AB—Carroll, Cruz, Eisenmann, Hummer, Parker; LH/SH—L. Swanson. Info: Lee Imes, P.O. Box 17361, Rochester, NY 14617; (716) 436-8141.

4-5 **Hauppauge, New York:** Paumanok CF (CFA). New York State Office Bldg., Long Island. Judges: AB—K. Everett, Gebhardt, Lee, Slodden, D. Swanson; LH/SH—Wawrzyn; LH—Petersen, Search; SH—Hymas-Thomas, Molino. Info: Russell Sawyer, RD 3, Box 116, Rt. 9W, Selkirk, NY 12158; (518) 767-9068.

4-5 **Elyria, Ohio:** North Coast CF (CFA). Elyria West High School, 42101 W. Griswold Rd. Judges: AB—Doernberg, C. Jensen, Roderick; LH/SH—L. Jensen, Prather; LH—Lawrence; SH—DeMercurio. Info: Pat Hudson, 39614 Parsons Rd., Grafton, OH 44044; (216) 926-2809.

4-5 **Spartanburg, South Carolina:** Foothills Felines (CFA). Spartanburg Memorial Auditorium. Judges: AB—Davis, Ehrhardt, Faulkner, Goltzer; LH/SH—Lindstrand, Wolfe. Info: Christine H. Fitch, 102 Carpenter Dr., Landrum, SC 29356; (803) 457-2768.

4-5 **Salt Lake City, Utah:** Promontory Point CC (CFA). Salt Palace. Judges: AB—Haussman, Kimball, Placchi, St. Georges; LH/SH—Dunn, R. Everett, Koepp, W. Thompson. Also HHP. Info: Charlene Carpenter, 297 E. 700 N., Kaysville, UT 84037; (801) 544-1994. EBCD: Jan. 15; CD: Feb. 17.

April 29-30, 1989 CFA
Daytona Beach Cat Fanciers
Daytona Beach, Fla.
Clarendon Hotel
Michael Brim
918 Millard Ct. West
Daytona Beach, Fla., 32017
(904) 258-7199

April 29-30, 1989 ACFA
Kacod Cat Club
Decatur, Ill.
Civic Center
Roy Spreckelmeyer
2495 N. Hill Lot 1
Decatur, Ill., 62526
(217) 877-1817

April 29-30, 1989 CFA
Sign of the Cat
Elizabeth, N.J.
Dun Sports Arena
Tony Laufnick
1 Oaktree Road
Saverville, N.J., 08872
(201) 738-7892

April 29-30, 1989 ACFA
Shenandoah Valley Cat Fanciers
Bridgewater, Va.
Andy Andruscavage
Route 2, Box 215
Dayton, Va., 22821
(703) 867-5733

The show calendar from *I Love Cats* magazine.
© 1989, Grass Roots Publishing Company, Inc.

Cat Fancy Magazine

Cat Fancy magazine has a section called "Show Calendar," which lists the upcoming shows. The following sample illustrates the information generally found therein.

As the calendar shows, on March 4 and 5, there is a show in Salt Lake City, Utah, sponsored by the Promontory Point Cat Club and sanctioned by CFA. It is being held at the Salt Palace. The All-Breed (AB) judges are listed along with the Specialty (longhair/shorthair) judges. Household Pets (HHP) are also being judged. A name, address and telephone number are listed for information. The Early Bird Closing Date (EBCD) is January 15 with the final Closing Date (CD) being February 17.

Cat Fancy
P.O. Box 6040
Mission Viejo, CA 92690

Cats Magazine

Cats magazine has a section called "To Show and Go," which has a schedule of shows by date. It also carries display ads for shows. The section often provides extensive information. For example, one issue notes that on March 3, 4 and 5 there is a show in New York City. It is being held at Madison Square Garden. Incats Garden CC (Cat Club) is the sponsoring club. The federation sanctioning the show is TICA. Following this information is a list of the judges who will be judging the show. One judge is still To Be Announced (TBA). The Entry Clerk (EC) is the person you would contact for further show information and entry forms. His name, address and telephone number are listed. The Early Bird Entry Fee (EBEF) is a discounted rate for entering the show if you enter by a certain date. The entry fees are given for Friday only, Saturday and Sunday together, and all three days. Following the EBEF is the price for entry if you choose not to enter by the early bird date. After the Early Bird Closing Date (EBCD), the early bird rates do not apply and you must pay the full fee to enter the show.

The announcements in *Cats* magazine are published in both of its editions (the regular edition and the exhibitors' edition. *Cats* requires that *all* show announcements be in by the fifteenth of the month, and that they arrive at least two months before the time the club wishes them to appear. If a club is late getting its announcement to the magazine, it may not be listed in time for you to enter the show.

BACK TO CATS

IS PROUD TO ANNOUNCE AN

ALLBREED CHAMPIONSHIP CAT SHOW

MARCH 25TH AND 26TH, 1989

AT THE HOLIDAY INN JETPORT IN ELIZABETH, NJ

SATURDAY JUDGES	SUNDAY JUDGES
Solveig Pflueger (AB)	Larry Paul (AB)
Steve Savant (AB)	Arthel Scheuermann (AB)
Larry Paul (SP)	LindaJean Grillo (AB)
LindaJean Grillo (SP)	Ann Hoehn (SP)
Robin Higgins (SP)	Robert Forte (SP)

ENTRY INFORMATION

Early Bird Entry Fees - Must be postmarked by February 11, 1989

Saturday or Sunday: $25.00 per entry   Both Days: $40.00 per entry

Regular Entry Fees - Must be received by March 11, 1989

Saturday or Sunday: $30.00 per entry   Both Days: $45.00 per entry

FINAL CLOSING DATE IS MARCH 11 OR WHEN 200 ENTRIES HAVE BEEN RECEIVED

See Summary Sheet for additional information and incidental fees. Please make checks payable to BACK TO CATS and include a summary sheet with your entry blank. All fees must accompany entries and are non-refundable. A service charge of $20.00 plus regular bank fees will be assessed on returned checks.

ENTRY CLERK
Bev Eitner
E-3 Richard Mine Rd
Wharton, NJ 07885
(201) 989-8366

INFORMATION
Alice Angermeyer
221 E. Columbia Ave.
Palisades Park, NJ 07650
(201) 945-4145

Vicky Depietro
240 Rockland Ave.
River Vale, NJ 07675
(201) 664-7604

PLEASE!! NO PHONE CALLS AFTER 10:00 P.M.!!

FOR INFORMATION ABOUT TICA OR REGISTERING YOUR CATS, CALL 1-800-TICA-INFO

Typical show flyers.

SUMMARY SHEET
BACK TO CATS
MARCH 25 AND 26, 1989

Please complete this form and return with entries and fees. Fee TOTALS must accompany entry forms. We will call you collect if significant questions arise regarding your entries. Make checks payable to BACK TO CATS and send to Bev Eitner, E-3 Richard Mine Rd, Wharton, NJ 07885-1807.

DESCRIPTION			AMOUNT
Early Bird Entries:	2 days	1 day (circle which day)	
(Postmarked by 02/11/89)	___ @ $40	___ @ $25 Sat Sun	$_____
Regular Entries:	2 days	1 day (circle which day)	
(Closes 03/11/89)	___ @ $45	___ @ $30 Sat Sun	$_____
Show Special Entries:	Three 2-day	$114	$_____
Show Special Entries:	Four 2-day	$150	$_____
Listing Fee (required for non-TICA registered adults in Championship and Alter classes)			
		$2.00 per cat per day	$_____
Sales Cage (1 adult or 2 kittens)		$20.00	$_____
Double Cage		$20.00	$_____
Guaranteed End-of-Row Benching		$10.00	$_____
Catalog ($4.00 at door)		$ 3.00	$_____
Substitutions (until closing date only)		$ 5.00	$_____
CATALOG ADVERTISING: B/W CAMERA-READY MUST BE PROVIDED BY CLOSING DATE			
	Full Page	$30.00	$_____
	Half Page	$20.00	$_____
	Quarter Page	$15.00	$_____
	Business Card	$ 5.00	$_____
EXHIBITOR'S SPECIAL - BUSINESS CARD		$ 2.00	$_____
Donation to rosette and ribbon fund		THANK YOU!!	$_____
		TOTAL	$_____

Check here if you are available to clerk   [   ] Saturday   Requested Judge: _____

                                   [   ] Sunday   Requested Judge: _____

Check here if you are available to steward [   ] Saturday   [   ] Sunday   Steward's name _____

EXHIBITOR'S NAME _____

ADDRESS _____

CITY _____ STATE _____ ZIP _____

HOME PHONE _____ WORK PHONE _____

LIBERTY TRAIL CAT FANCIERS

PRESENTS
A 6 RING CFA CHAMPIONSHIP SHOW
OCTOBER 28-29, 1989
DUNN SPORT CENTER
ELIZABETH, N.J

OUR JUDGES

Larry Adkison ALLBREED   Wayne Trevathan ALLBREED   Craig Rothermel ALLBREED
Donna Jean Thompson LH/SH SPECIALTY   Nancy Dodds LH/SH SPECIALTY
Joan O'Hara LH SPECIALTY   Hilary Helmrich SH SPECIALTY

SHOW MANAGER: *Jill Archibald 47 Hudson St. Freehold, NJ 07728*
ENTRY CLERK: *Tony Laufnick 1 Oaktree Rd. Sayreville, NJ 08872*
(201) 238-7892 *NO CALLS AFTER 10PM*

CLOSING DATE: OCTOBER 16, 1989 FIRM!!!

ENTRY FEES:
$31.00 *Each* 1st 2 Entries $21.00 *Each* Addt'l Entry (SAME OWNER)
$10.00 Dbl/Sales Cage $5.00 End of Row 6$ Substitution fee
All entry fees include $1 for North Atlantic Region

All entries must be submitted on the official CFA Entry blank, accompanied by the proper fees. CFA registration numbers must be included for all Championship and Premiership classes. Kittens must be four months old by the date of the show. Make checks payable to LIBERTY TRAIL CAT FANCIERS. A fee of $20.00 will be charged for any checks returned by the bank.

STARTING TIME: The show hall will open at 8AM on Saturday and all cats must be benched by 9:30AM or they will be marked absent. Judging will begin promptly at 10AM on Saturday and 9:30AM on Sunday. All entries must remain in the show hall until 4PM unless permission is received from the show manager.

Cages are approximately 22'X22"X22". Cat food, litter and litter pans will be provided. People food will be available. No vet inspection prior to benching is required. All entries should be inoculated against feline enteritis, rhinotracheitis and calici viruses and tested for FelV by a licensed vet. Cats should be free of mites, fleas and fungus. CFA rules require that your cat's front and back claws be clipped.

Our show is held under the auspices of the Cat Fanciers Association. CFA show rules will be strictly enforced. A copy of the rules is available from CFA, 1309 Allaire Avenue, Ocean, N.J. 07712. The club reserves the right to add judges not named in the show announcement to judge non-championship and non-premiership classes. All championship, premiership and registered kittens will be scored for CFA National and Regional awards.

Cats will not be permitted in the show hall overnight. The club will exercise due care on the sponsorship of this show, but will not be liable for any losses, damage or injury. No watchman will be provided during the hours the show is not open.

DIRECTIONS & ACCOMODATIONS: Our show hall is the Dunn Sport Center, Elizabeth, NJ. It is climate controlled and SMOKING IS NOT PERMITTED. Detailed directions and hotel information will be sent with the confirmation.

Cats
P.O. Box 83048
Lincoln, NE 68501

I Love Cats

This magazine has a section called "Show Time" with limited information about shows.

As the sample *I Love Cats* calendar on p. 42 shows, on April 29 and 30, an ACFA-sanctioned show will be sponsored by the Shenandoah Valley Cat Fanciers of Bridgewater, Virginia. For information, you should contact the person listed.

I Love Cats
Grass Roots Publishing Company, Inc.
950 Third Avenue
New York, NY 10022

Cat World™ *International*

This magazine, published primarily for breeders and active exhibitors, claims to have the fancy's most comprehensive show listing.

As a *Cat World*™ *International* calendar would show, on April 15, 1989, a CFF sanctioned show will be held in Portland, Maine. It will be held in the gym of the University of Southern Maine, and is sponsored by the Downeast Cat Club. There will be three All-Breed and two Specialty rings. The judges are listed. In addition, a contact person for information about the show is listed along with her address and telephone number.

Cat World™ *International*
P.O. Box 35635
Phoenix, AZ 85069-5635

FEDERATION PUBLICATIONS

Publications of the federations, either those that are a part of your membership, such as *TICA Trends* (TICA), or those you can get by subscription, such as *Cat Fanciers' Almanac* (CFA), will list the show schedule for that federation only. This schedule is usually a very extensive one. For that reason, the show information or the show itself may change. Also, new shows are always being added.

A pamphlet from CFA may help you to determine your cat's color. © *1989 CFA.*

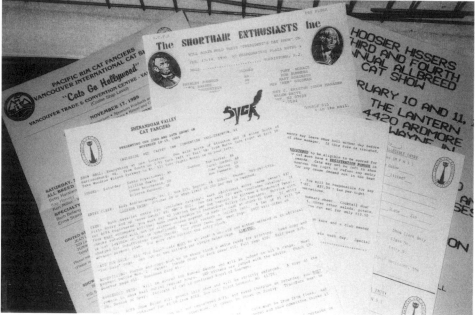

When you exhibit at a cat show, you will get flyers about other shows that the association is sanctioning.

800 NUMBERS

TICA has a service for getting information on shows scheduled through the use of an 800 telephone number. For show information, call 1-800-TICA-INF. You will be talking to a person, not a recording, who has the latest information on scheduled TICA shows.

SHOW FLYERS

At every show, many flyers are handed out with information about forthcoming shows of that federation. These are usually put on the top of the exhibitor cages. If you attend a show as a spectator and want a show flyer, an exhibitor may be able to direct you to the cat club representatives who are handing out the flyers.

4

Preparation
and Grooming

YOU SHOULD START preparing your cat for a show as soon as you decide to enter. If you buy a kitten and know you are going to show it, prepare the kitten for a show career from the time you bring it home.

HEALTH

Before you start socializing your cat, you must make certain it is clean and healthy. The cat should be wormed, all shots should be up to date, and the cat should test "negative" for Feline Leukemia Virus. Make sure your cat is free of fleas, mites, fungus, parasites and other pests.

A show cat should be in *top* condition overall. Top condition starts with the best nutrition. Because cat shows are stressful for the cat as well as the exhibitor, you might consider supplementing your cat's food with a vitamin compound while it is being shown, even if you don't do this every day at home. Since many cats eat less than usual during a cat show, make certain the food is the best quality and is nutritionally complete. If your cat loses a little weight because of the shows, you can feed it a cat food that is higher in calories than the normal food or you can supplement its food with a high-calorie, multivitamin preparation.

Needless to say, if your cat begins to demonstrate too many genuine signs of stress, you should not show. Some cats never adapt to the life of the show ring. Most of them will, as long as you make it a fun experience for them.

SOCIALIZATION

Now that your cat's health requirements are taken care of, you should begin socialization. Your cat probably doesn't socialize as much as you do. At a cat show, there will be smells from many other cats, including whole males, and many people looking into the cage. The showhall itself can be noisy and very crowded. Cats will also have to be handled by judges who will examine them in a specific way for specific characteristics. They must get used to this handling. If a judge cannot handle your cat, disqualification from the ring may result.

Begin socialization by picking up your cat and putting it on a smooth surface, such as a drainboard or table so you can examine it as the judge will. Have the cat stand while you check ears, face, fur, tail and any special characteristics for the breed. For example, Japanese Bobtails will have the tail examined by the judge for the bone structure underlying the puff of fur. In examining a Persian, the judge will feel the "break" between the nose and the eyes. Be certain your cat gets used to having fingers on its face, its fur brushed backward, its tail felt, its ears touched, and its legs and stance checked.

In order to check the face and the eye color of the cat, the judge will hold the cat up in front of his or her face. If artificial lights are being used for judging, the cat may have a bright light in its eyes as the judge turns around, so make certain your cat is used to bright lights.

If your cats seem unhappy about being handled this way, follow your handling and examination with a little play time and, perhaps, a cat treat. Over time, they will associate this with having fun.

After your cat is used to your examination, have someone you know come over and examine it the same way. After the exam, again give your cat some play time or a treat. As you continue this socialization, stop giving treats every time your cat is examined. After a while, your cat will accept this exam as part of its life.

If you will be showing an HHP, you must get the cat used to the same procedure. While HHPs have no characteristics that are breed-specific, they are examined just as thoroughly as purebred cats, and in the same way. Since some judges, although not all, take into account the character of the HHP in their judging, you will want to make certain your HHP is cooperative while being judged and does not hiss or growl.

SGC Edmars Allison waits patiently on the grooming table.

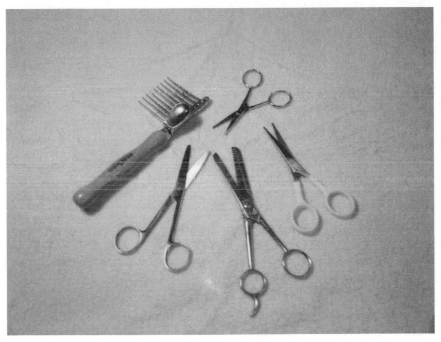

An assortment of tools used for grooming and trimming.

Use the same method described above to get your HHP ready for the show ring, including the use of a cat treat, if you wish.

CAGING

If your cats have never been caged before, you might also want to get them used to cages. If you don't have a cat cage at home, use the cage you will be using to transport the cat to the show. When you put the cat in the cage, put a treat in the cage. After a while, eliminate the treat. When you cage your cat in the judging ring, you can put a treat in the cage there also. When removing the cat from the ring, remember to take the treat out of the cage if it has not been eaten. It may also be helpful to get your cat used to the cage when it is sleepy. Sometimes the desire to sleep will overcome any initial nervousness your cat may have when it is first caged.

While your cat is in the cage, play with it. Use its favorite toy, or play with it by rubbing a feather or a tassel toy across the cage bars. Most cats will have fun trying to catch this toy. During judging, you may find that the judge uses this trick to attract the cat's attention.

GROOMING YOUR CAT

Grooming for the show ring is different from the everyday grooming you do. Extremely beneficial for your cat, it takes into account all the parts of the animal. For several reasons, a cat that is shown is generally in better condition, despite the added stress of the shows, than a cat that is not shown. A show cat is kept in the best shape nutritionally, its weight is maintained at the optimal level, its coat is brushed and is free of knots, its teeth are scraped and brushed regularly, and, while being bathed, its entire body is felt and examined. If anything is wrong with your cat, you will know it immediately.

When grooming, make yourself comfortable. Proper grooming takes time. Don't expect to spend much less time on a shorthair cat than on a longhair. The proper grooming of a shorthair cat can take almost as much time as grooming a longhair.

Wear comfortable clothes that are no problem when they get wet. Since your cat will be wet, make sure the grooming area is keep warm and free of drafts. Get all your equipment out at the beginning and keep it easily available. Most cats will not just sit there quietly while you go get the tooth scraper that you left in the other room.

Nail clippers should be sharp and comfortable for the groomer to use.

Be careful not to cut the pink "quick," as this can result in bleeding. Most problems with nail cutting occur because the groomer is nervous.

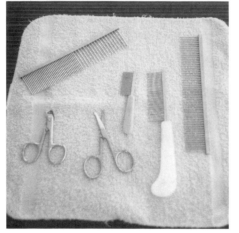

Several combs of varying sizes may be used to groom one longhair cat.

Nail Clipping

Begin your grooming session by clipping the cat's nails. All cat shows require that the cats' nails, on all four paws, be clipped before the show. If cats become nervous, afraid or annoyed, they might try to claw the judge. Needless to say, the judge wants to avoid this. Sometimes, at a show, you will see and hear a cat who get spooked and tries to attack the judge. Some judges have been severely hurt this way. At least clipped claws help stop some of this. Then the judge just has to make sure the cat doesn't bite.

When clipping your cat's nails:

- Invest in a very good-quality pair of nail clippers specifically made for clipping the nails of cats. Have them professionally sharpened or replace them if they appear to have become dull.
- Always clip nails under good light so that you can differentiate between the nail and the pink "quick." The quick will bleed if you cut it and cause pain to the cat.
- Hold the cat, take a paw in your hand and gently press the pad to extend the nails.
- Look at the nail from the side to see the quick. If you look at the bottom, you will see dirt that is under the nail and may misjudge how much is to be cut.
- Cut the nail below the quick as short as you can.
- Repeat on all nails.

Most difficulties with nail clipping tend to be caused by the discomfort of the groomer, not the cat. If you are nervous, your cat will pick up the nervousness and may struggle, causing the entire nail-clipping session to become unnecessarily difficult for everyone involved. The purpose of clipping the nails for a show is to ensure that the cat will not hurt anyone. If all you feel comfortable clipping is the very sharp ends of the claws, then let it go at that and try to do a closer job of clipping every time you do it. Keep a bottle of styptic powder at hand when you clip nails in case you inadvertently cause some bleeding. Put it on the bleeding claw immediately and the bleeding will stop.

Some cats, especially the oriental breeds, are extremely sensitive to touch and may not like having their paws handled. If this is the case, play with the cat after you handle each paw and make the session a fun experience for the cat.

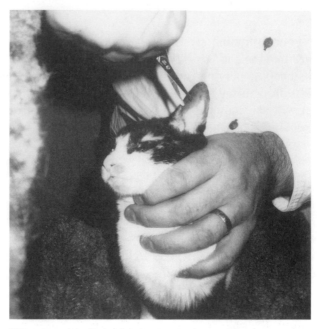

Kiri, a Japanese Bobtail, is having the fur in her ears trimmed to accentuate the height of the ear itself. A small, curved scissor is used for the trimming.

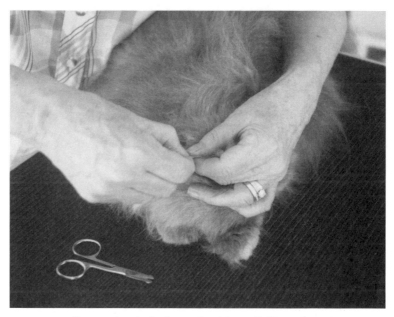

Ears can be plucked as well as trimmed with a scissor.

Trimming

It is beneficial to highlight specific characteristics on purebred cats so that judges notice them in the ring. For that reason, some careful trimming may be needed. For example, the inside tufts of fur are trimmed from the ears of a Japanese Bobtail to accentuate the height of the ears, while the line of fur on the top of the ears on a Persian is trimmed to accentuate the smallness of the Persian's ears.

The best way to learn how to groom a specific breed of cat is to talk to the breeder who sold you your cat and to others who show the breed you are showing. Most breeders are happy to share grooming tips with those just starting to exhibit. Every breeder has special techniques for grooming, however, so don't hesitate to talk to a couple of exhibitors, especially if you like the way they have groomed the cat they are showing. Eventually, you will develop your own style of grooming. Then remember to help others who ask you for grooming hints.

For general trimming:

- Use small, curved grooming scissors. Keep them well sharpened.
- Under a strong light, with the curved side of the scissors up and away from the skin of the cat, trim slowly and carefully.
- Do not attempt to trim your cats if they are too feisty or playful. Wait until they are sleepy and trim then.

Some groomers choose to pluck the fur instead of cutting it. This gives a much smoother line in the area plucked. However, plucking can leave a pore open, which may later become infected. If you do pluck hairs from your cat, be certain that the area is kept clean.

Some groomers, especially those who have experience grooming dogs, use an electric grooming razor for their trimming. If you are careful, this can be a quick and effective method of trimming. Be certain to get your cat used to the noise of the razor before you trim with it.

When it comes to HHPs, trimming is not usually done. What makes a purebred cat out of line with the Standard can be extremely appealing on a HHP. For example, if you have a longhaired, Persian-type HHP with extremely long ear tufts, you have something special. Small ears on a shorthair cat can also make for a very winning look. While HHPs must be clean and groomed the same way a purebred cat is groomed, the natural, untrimmed look is usually much more interesting than a carefully trimmed look.

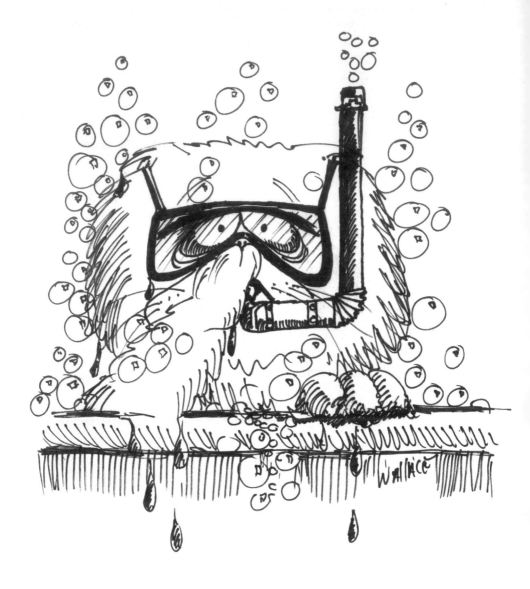

Bathing

We talked to one judge about what advice he would give a first-time exhibitor. He said that many first-time exhibitors will show a dirty cat. Needless to say, a dirty cat will not make the Finals in that condition. In fact, bathing is more than just cosmetic. It is a matter of health. For example, if a judge finds evidence of fleas on your cat, the cat may even be disqualified from the show.

Getting Your Cat Used to Water

All cats will need a bath sometime in their lives. Most cats are not really opposed to water. In fact, some of them even swim or take showers with their owners. But the best thing to do with a cat you will be showing is to get it used to water. The easiest way to get your cat used to being bathed is to start when the cat is a young kitten. Fill a clean sink or washpan with very warm water and let the kitten get used to having a small area of its body washed. With most kittens, the area that first needs washing is the hindquarters.

Next, let your kitten stand in the water. Let some water from the spigot or a spray nozzle run into the sink or wash pan. At this point, the kitten should be ready for a complete bath.

Most cats get used to bathing fairly easily. As long as you can make this a fun experience, the cat will not be afraid. Talk to your cat during the bath and play after the cat is dry. You may also want to reward the cat with a treat after a bath.

If your cat gets very frightened during a bath and begins to struggle, grab it firmly by the scruff of the neck. This should stop the struggling. Talk calmly and quietly, then attempt to resume the bath. If your cat tries to leave the sink or tub, you can wash it while the cat is wearing a nylon figure-eight harness.

Some cats are uncomfortable in the sink or tub because they have little or no traction on such a smooth surface. You can overcome this by placing a rubber mat in the sink. For some cats, even this is not enough. If the rubber mat does not provide a comfortable footing for your cat, you can put a window screen in the bottom of the tub. This screening gives your cat something to cling to and may help it feel comfortable.

You may want to consider getting your cat used to being bathed in a tub or under the shower. From time to time, you may find that your cat has to be bathed away from home before a show. Unless you have planned ahead and brought a portable diverter for the sink, you will have to wash your cat in the tub or under the shower.

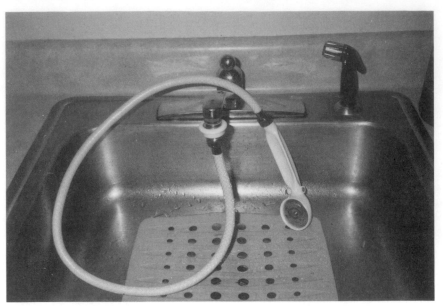

A hose with a spray nozzle turns a kitchen sink into a cat bathtub.

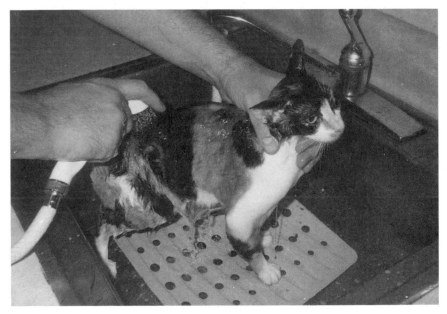

A rubber mat provides a good surface for the cat during the bath.

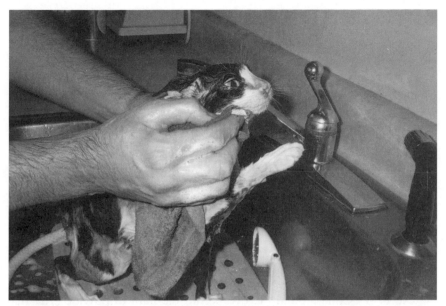

Use a washcloth for the face.

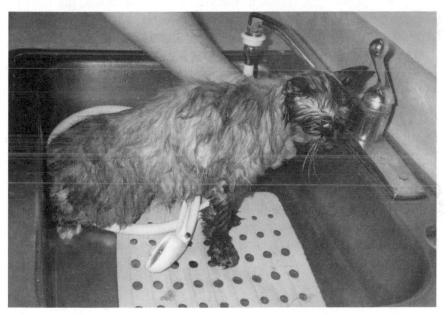

SGM Priscilla's Bouquet ("Gaiety") enjoys her bath.

Bathing Tips

Because you want the bath to be a comfortable experience for your cat, you should follow a few simple rules. First, make certain the room temperature is warm enough for your cat while it is being bathed and toweled off. Bath towels are easily heated by placing them in the clothes dryer for a few minutes before they are used on the cat. In addition to the air temperature, be certain the water temperature is warm enough for your cat. Cats have higher body temperatures than humans do, so the water should be a little warmer than you might use for yourself.

A longhair cat should be brushed before being bathed to make certain that there are no knots or tangles. When you bathe your cat, you will be pulling your fingers through the fur. This can be very uncomfortable for the cat if you keep running into tangles.

Try to keep the shampoo out of your cat's eyes and ears. Most cat shampoos are tearless, but you still don't want to risk making your cat uncomfortable by getting soap in its eyes. Some people put eyedrops in the eye or Vaseline around the eye before the bath to provide a barrier to the soap in case it does happen to run toward the eye. Whether you choose to do this or not, be very careful washing the face. In fact, you may want to wash the face during the bath with a washcloth, as this can make it easier to control the soaping and rinsing process.

Some people put cotton in the ears of the cat before the bath to prevent water and shampoo from entering the ear canal. However, this can cause more problems than benefits. The cotton can muffle the hearing of the cat and make a cat spooky. You also have to make sure you remove all the cotton without leaving a filament in the ear, which can cause problems later.

Prewash

Longhair cats that need to look especially puffy, shorthair cats that develop a lot of oil on their coat and cats that have not been bathed in a while will benefit from a prewash treatment. Any prewash preparation you use should be made specifically for cats. Never use a degreaser that is made for humans to wash grease and oil from their hands as it may cause an allergic reaction in cats. For effective prewash:

- Use a spray nozzle and very warm water and wet your cat thoroughly. Completely wetting a longhair cat or a shorthair cat with a thick coat can take time, but the cat must be *completely* wet before you proceed. Since the outer coat will act as a barrier to getting the undercoat wet, separate the fur by running your fingers through it and allow the water to get all the way to the skin.

- When the cat is thoroughly wet, use the prewash in the dilution recommended on the bottle just as you would use a shampoo.
- Use the prewash on all parts of the cat, but concentrate particularly on the back and sides where the cat will be handled. Also concentrate on areas where cats tends to look most greasy—for example, the area on the back of the tail, which is the location of the supra-caudal gland. On some mature male cats this area may show evidence of an excessive accumulation of oil and grease known as "stud tail."
- Rinse the prewash out completely.

Shampoo

Use only shampoos made specifically for cats. *Never* use any products sold as degreasing dish detergents, as these have been known to cause allergic reactions in cats.

- Use shampoo in the dilution recommended on the bottle and lather the cat thoroughly.
- Take special care to wash between the toes of the cat, the hind-quarters, the belly and the entire tail.
- Wash the face carefully along with the chin and neck, using a washcloth, if you can handle it easily. While most shampoos that are made for cats are tearless, you still don't want to get any soap in the eyes of the cat. If you get soap in your cat's eyes, rinse it out immediately with warm water and follow with a neutral eye-drop.
- Rinse thoroughly and repeat the shampoo.

Cream Rinses and Conditioners

Some exhibitors use cream rinses or conditioners on the cat to enhance the feel of the fur. They can also be helpful to prevent dryness if the cat is being bathed often. If you choose to use a cream rinse or conditioner, use only products made specifically for use on cats and follow the dilution directions on the bottle.

Since a cream rinse that makes a Burmese cat look beautiful can make a Devon Rex look greasy, always try out any new product at a time when you will not be showing the cat. See how the cat looks and

Even though the shampoo you use may be tearless, be certain not to get any shampoo in the cat's eyes.

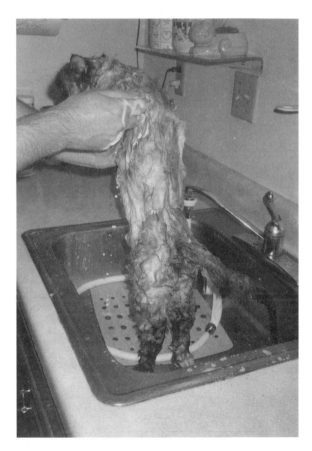

All the shampoo must be thoroughly rinsed out of the cat's coat.

how long the effect lasts. That way, when you are grooming your cat for a show, you will know exactly what to use.

Vinegar Rinses

After you thoroughly rinse the shampoo out of the cat's fur, you might want to follow with a vinegar rinse. This helps to remove any shampoo left in the coat. However, it is not an alternative to a complete and thorough job of rinsing. If you are using a vinegar rinse:

- Dilute one tablespoon of white vinegar in one quart of warm water.
- Pour the mixture on the cat's fur, keeping the solution away from the cat's face.
- Massage the vinegar rinse into the coat.
- Rinse the cat with warm water. If you rinse completely, the smell of the vinegar will not remain on the cat.

After you have finished rinsing your cat, rub your hand down the fur, getting as much water out of the coat as you can. Wrap the cat in a big, absorbent towel, preferably one that has been warmed. When the cat is all bundled up, rub it all over with the towel without removing it. At this point, many cats will take a nap in your arms.

Special Preparations

Whiteners and lightening shampoos are special shampoos specifically made to whiten white-haired cats and lighten light-colored cats. Follow directions on the product bottle and rinse thoroughly, as these shampoos are very thick. The whitening shampoos are generally purple or dark blue and the lightening shampoos are usually pastels of the same colors.

Special shampoos are also made to enhance the color of black, brown and other dark-haired cats. Follow all directions and rinse thoroughly.

Conditioning shampoos have a conditioner built into the shampoo. They eliminate the need for a separate conditioner.

Texturizing shampoos are for cats that have little or no undercoat. They enhance the feel of the fur.

Some skin problems are treated with the use of medicated shampoos. Shampoos are also made to combat fleas and fungus problems such as ringworm. These products should be used under supervision of a veterinarian. If you are going to use a medicated shampoo as a preventive

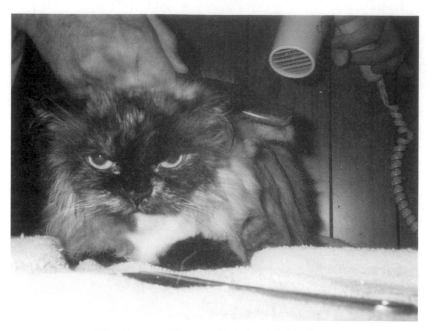

When the coat dries completely, brush it into place.

A drying cage can be used for a shorthair cat.

measure, or after a cat show, be sure you test it first on a small area of the cat. If your cat does not show signs of being allergic to the product, you should be able to use it safely.

Rinse very, very thoroughly. This is not easy with a longhair cat, but it is very important. A shampoo film on the fur of the cat makes a bad appearance. More important, your cat may ingest this residue when it licks itself and this can cause internal problems.

Drying Your Cat

Your cat will be dried differently depending upon coat length. No matter what the length, however, make certain your cat is *completely* dry before you let it run around.

No matter what kind of cat you are grooming, as soon as you let go, the cat is bound to find some way to get dirty. If you have more than one cat, this is the time they will wrestle around together, ripping out large hunks of fur. Aside from confining cats, there seems to be nothing you can do about this.

Using a Blow Dryer

Longhair cats are best dried with a hand-held blow dryer. You can purchase dryers that are made especially for grooming animals. However, since they are expensive and made for the professional groomer who may be grooming many large dogs or cats each day, most exhibitors will just use a blow dryer made for people. We suggest that you look for one with several heat settings and a filter you can clean.

At first, your cat may not like the whine produced by the dryer. However, if you take the time, your cat will soon get used to the sound of the dryer. In fact, some cats learn to like the sound very quickly, because they associate the sound with the owner paying a lot of attention to them.

With your cat on the grooming table, blow the coat backward, using your fingers to ruffle it so you can get down to the skin. As each area dries, brush upward and back in place. Do not brush the fur when it is wet as this may damage or break it. Be certain to dry the entire tail and the fur on the legs, on the belly and under the forelegs. By the time your cat is dry, the coat should have been thoroughly brushed.

The Drying Cage

Using a blow dryer on a shorthair cat may disturb the way the coat should lie. For this reason, many exhibitors do not use dryers on shorthair

cats, but prefer a drying cage. A drying cage is one in which you can confine your cat while drying. Put a small space heater by the cage to provide warmth so your cat does not get a cold or a draft while drying. A space heater that blows warm air is fine. There should not be so much air current that it disarranges the line of the coat as it dries. Once your cat is used to the drying cage, it will probably take a nap while drying.

Do not put the dryer in the cage. The space heater may have exposed elements that can burn your cat. Even a hot air dryer can get very hot to the touch.

When completely dry, remove the cat from the cage and brush with a soft or a rubber brush. This will help to take any loose fur out of the coat. After you have brushed, smooth the coat down with a chamois cloth. This shines the fur and makes the cat look very silky.

Professional Groomers

Some professional groomers will groom cats. In fact, some of them specialize in cat grooming. The use of professional groomers is not necessary in order to exhibit cats. In fact, most exhibitors do not use a professional groomer, prefering to do the grooming themselves. However, if you want to have your cat groomed professionally, you should first get recommendations from friends who use a groomer or from your vet. When making an appointment, be certain to ask if the groomer has any experience grooming cats.

Alternatives to Bathing

Sometimes a cat will just not tolerate being bathed no matter what you do. You can still prepare this cat for a show by using products that do not require a full soaking bath.

Dry shampoos are available for cat cleaning. To use these, sprinkle the powder on the cat and brush it out. It must be brushed out *completely*, however, because the residue can make a cat that licks it off sick.

Liquid preparations are used in various ways depending upon how dirty the cat is. If your cat needs only a light cleaning, you can apply the product in a misting bottle and towel dry. If you need a medium cleaning, soak a washcloth with the preparation and rub it on against the lay of the hair. Rub with a towel until the coat is dry. If the cat needs a more thorough cleaning, apply the preparation directly from the bottle and work it into a lather. Then towel dry the cat.

If you use one of these preparations instead of giving your cat a

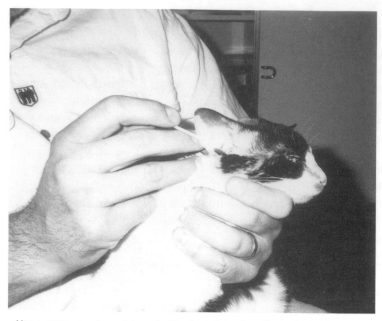

Use a cotton swab, moistened with alcohol, to clean the inside of the ears.

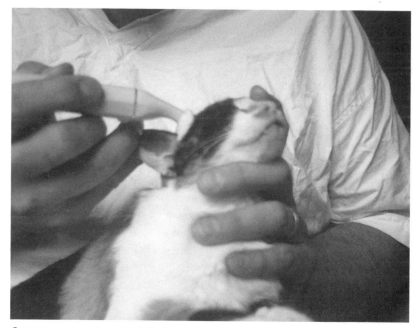

Groomers who are comfortable handling an electric razor can also use it to trim the ears.

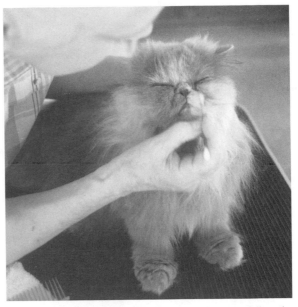

If you use a special preparation to clean the eyes, follow the instructions precisely.

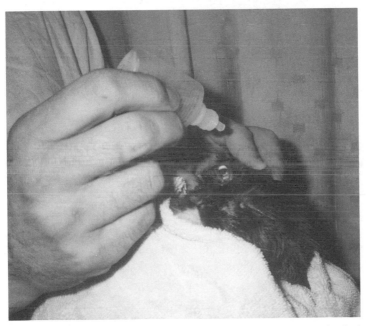

Liquid tears may be used after the bath to wash out any soap or water that may have entered the cat's eye.

bath, follow your cleaning with the rest of the grooming preparations described below.

The Ears

With your cat bundled up in a towel, you are now ready to clean the inside of the ears. *This is very important, as the judge can spot a dirty ear right away. Even if the ear is dirty with ear wax, the judge may wonder if the cat has ear mites. This can disqualify the cat from the show.* To clean ears:

- Dampen a cotton swab with alcohol or baby oil and carefully clean the inside of the cat's ears. Be careful not to go too far into the canal of the ear.
- If the ears are especially dirty, pour a *small* amount of hydrogen peroxide inside the ear canal. Let it stay in for a minute, then blot it out with tissues and cotton swabs.

The Eyes

When you have finished with the ears, clean the eyes. Some breeds of cat, primarily those with flat faces, have tear stains on their faces. This is not always an indication that the cat is sick, teary-eyed or unclean. It can just be more apparent because of the color of the cat, or it may be congenital, according to the line of the cat.

For gentle but effective eye cleaning:

- Moisten the end of a washcloth or cotton ball with warm water or a special preparation made for cleaning cats' eyes.
- Carefully clean the area around the eyes with the washcloth or cotton. There are preparations that are made specifically to clean up tear stains from around the eyes. These are usually applied with a cotton ball and then wiped off with a dry cotton ball. If your cat has problems with tear stains, you might consider using a product for this problem. When using a specialized product, follow all directions carefully.
- Always use a separate cotton ball for each eye. If you are using a washcloth, use a separate section of the washcloth for each eye. This prevents introducing contaminants from one eye to the other.
- To clear out any soap that may have entered the eye during the shampoo, put two drops of plain eyedrops or liquid tears in each eye.

74

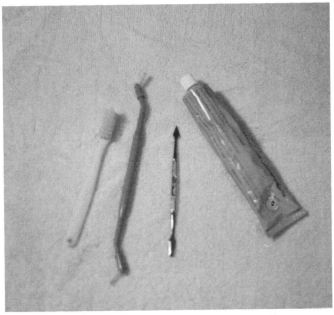

Proper dental care is critical to your cat's health.

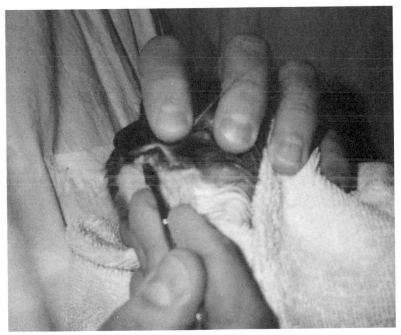

Scrape the canines before you brush the teeth.

The Nose

Cats get dirty noses just like children. It can't blow its nose, and it can't cover its nose and mouth when it sneezes. For these reasons, you will have to clean the nose for your cat. To do this:

- Moisten the end of a washcloth or a cotton ball with warm water.
- Carefully clean the nose leather.
- Clean the nostrils, making certain you do not enter them very far.

The Teeth

Dental care is very important in maintaining your cat's good health. A thorough tooth cleaning should be performed by a veterinarian every year. Your show grooming will not replace that. However, a cat who is being shown must have clean teeth and good breath. For that reason, good oral hygiene can be maintained by routine scraping and brushing. You can scrape your cat's teeth by:

- Opening your cat's mouth, exposing the teeth.
- Using the flat side of your tooth scraper and scraping the canine teeth (the ''fangs'') in a downward motion from the gumline to the end of the tooth. Do not use too much pressure. If you scrape your cat's teeth regularly, you will not see a large buildup of plaque.
- Wiping the tooth off with the end of a washcloth dipped in warm water.
- Scraping the other major teeth in the same manner. Usually your cat's mouth is small, as are the teeth, and the only teeth you will be able to scrape are the large ones on the top and bottom.

The size of your cat's mouth will determine the size brush you will need for effective toothbrushing. For a large mouth you will be able to use an infant- or child-sized brush. If your cat has a small mouth, buy an eyebrow brush or a small brush specifically made for cleaning between the teeth.

The toothpaste you should use is one made just for animals. Such toothpastes are available at pet stores or at your vet's office. To brush your cat's teeth:

- Open the cat's mouth, exposing the teeth.
- Using a small amount of toothpaste, gently brush all the teeth that you can reach easily without gagging your cat or making it uncomfortable.

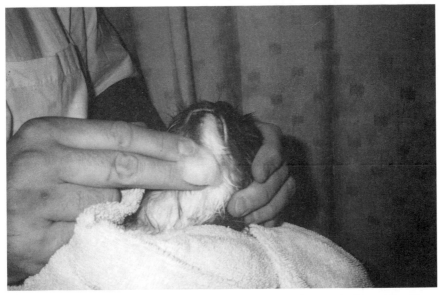

Cat acne can be a problem in any breed, but it is easy to spot on a cat with a white chin.

After drying your shorthair cat, brush it with a rubber brush and "polish" it with a chamois cloth.

- Since cat toothpaste is meant to be left on the teeth, there is no need to wipe off the toothpaste.

The Chin

A common problem is cat acne. Small blackheads can form on the chin and will be apparent upon close examination, particularly the kind a judge will do.

Sometimes feeding your cat in a flat, rather than a deep, dish is helpful in preventing cat acne. If your cat is a particularly messy eater or is lazy when it comes to washing itself, you might want to clean the chin after feeding. Cat acne can be very apparent on a cat with a white chin. If cat acne becomes too severe, the blackheads can open and become infected. Then the cat must be treated by a veterinarian. To prevent cat acne:

- Check the chin closely for any sign of blackheads or white pustules.
- Clean the chin with the end of a washcloth dipped in warm water.
- After cleaning the chin, wipe it carefully with a cotton ball dipped in alcohol. Be certain to penetrate the fur and get down to the skin.

IMPORTANT REMINDERS

No matter who suggests it, whether an exhibitor or a professional groomer, *never* use bleach or hair dye on a cat. Bleaches and hair dyes, even those for use on human facial hair, are tested for safety only on humans, not for safety on cats. Even if someone recommends bleaching or using hair dye and that person tells you he or she has never had a problem with it, your cat might be the one that has an allergic reaction. This reaction can range from having the hair fall out of the area that was bleached or dyed to convulsions or even death. Besides being unsafe, the use of bleach or hair dyes on cats is not condoned by any cat federation and this practice has no place in the showhall. In fact, if an exhibitor is found to have used bleach or hair dye on a cat he or she is exhibiting, most federations will expel the exhibitor from the showhall, if not from membership in the federation itself.

Never use any product on a cat that has not been made specifically for use on cats. This is your only assurance of safety. That something can be used safely on people does not mean it is automatically safe to

When the cat is dry, brush the entire coat to be sure it is free of knots and tangles.

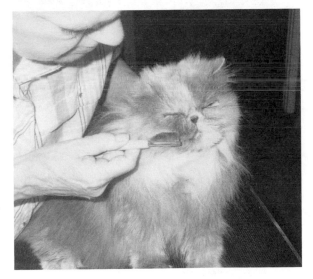

A small comb may be used to finish grooming the face.

A beautifully groomed Persian is a magnificent cat.

use on cats. Some cats are severely allergic to ingredients used in human soaps, cleaners and even cosmetics. Also, remember, a product that is safe for humans was probably not tested for safety for consumption, and that is what your cat may do with it when it cleans its fur after you have used it. Don't listen to anyone who tells you to just use a dishwashing product or a soap used to clean furniture. It is not any cheaper than using safe products, and it may result in your cat having an allergic reaction to chemicals in the product.

5

Entry Procedures

Every show has an Entry Clerk, either an individual or a company that does Entry Clerk work professionally, usually designated in the show materials as EC. The Entry Clerk is in charge of answering questions, providing you with information on the show and processing your entry. This is the first person you contact about the show. If your request or question should be answered by another show official, the Entry Clerk will provide you with the name and number of the person to contact.

The Entry Clerk has a difficult and time-consuming job. You don't want to make it even more difficult, so be certain you always *print or type* your entry, as it must be readable to be processed.

Always follow the directions given in the show flyer on how to contact the Entry Clerk. For example, some individuals may only be contacted by telephone in the evening. If the Entry Clerk is a professional service, it may have only daytime hours. Since Entry Clerks are also exhibitors, do not expect to be able to get in touch with them on a weekend. Also, never ask an Entry Clerk to violate federation or club rules—for example, by requesting that he or she accept a postdated check.

The most common error made in entering a show is to make the entry fee check out to the wrong person. Entry fees are usually paid to the club sponsoring the show, unless otherwise specified in the show flyer.

If you are having trouble filling out an entry form, the Entry Clerk can help you. If you are showing a Household Pet for the first time and are not sure of the correct classification, enclose a photograph of the cat along with a note explaining your difficulty in classifying the cat. If you have a purebred cat registered in the federation sanctioning the show you wish to enter, but the registration form has not come back by the time you fill in the entry form, list the registration as "pending." If the registration comes back before the show, call the Entry Clerk with the registration number to try to get it into the catalog.

THE SHOW FLYER

Show flyers list almost all the information needed to enter any show sponsored by a major federation. Among the essentials included are:

- The name of the sponsoring federation.
- The name of the show-giving club.
- The date.
- Specialty judges.
- All-Breed judges.
- The name of the Entry Clerk, with phone.
- The name of the show manager, with phone.

Along with these particulars, the location of the show is listed. Detailed directions will be sent with your entry confirmation. The size of the showhall and whether it is climate-controlled are indicated. This is important, as some showhalls are not climate-controlled, which can be very hard on longhair cats in the summer.

The flyer also tells you how many cats can be entered at this show. The entry fee is given (note that Household Pets have separate information for some shows), as well as the closing date by which you must enter this show.

In order for you to show a kitten, the kitten must be four months old at the time of the show. If you are selling kittens, the number of kittens to a cage is limited and you must pay a fee for the kittens' cage. If you want a double cage (two single cages opened up together to make one large cage) for just one cat, you must pay an additional fee. The check is made payable to the sponsoring cat club.

If you enter a cat, and then change your mind about showing that cat and decide to show another cat in its place, you are making a substitution. You may make a substitution only up until the closing date of the show, and you will have to pay an additional fee.

A benching request is a special request to be benched next to a specific exhibitor. Benching requests cannot always be honored, so if you are not benched next to the person you requested, it may have been something the club was just not able to do.

Household Pets information is specific only to HHPs. In some cases, there will be a limit on the number of HHPs allowed in the show and, because of the limit, instead of giving recognition to ten cats per judging ring, only five cats may be in the finals. The entry fee for HHPs may differ from the regular entry fee. HHPs must be spayed or neutered if they are adults and they cannot be declawed.

The flyer will indicate the time that you must check into the showhall for benching. If you don't check in at this time, you will be marked absent. Although there may not be a mandatory check of the cats by a veterinarian before a show, the cats should have all their shots up to date and their claws must be clipped.

Since there may not be a guard at the showhall overnight, you might want to take any valuables you have in the showhall out of the hall for the night.

The advertising section names a contact person for those breeders who might wish to advertise their cattery in the show catalog or for vendors who may wish to rent a booth at the show.

The cage and supplies section mentions that cat food, litter, boxes and dishes will be provided for the cats. If your cat likes only certain food, be sure to bring your own. The cage size is given so that you can adequately cover the cage. This also helps you to decide if you need a double cage for one entry. If your cat will feel cramped living in a space that is twenty-two by twenty-two by twenty-four inches for two days, get a double cage. A double cage for one entry will be twenty-two by forty-four by twenty-four inches.

Accommodations listings give the names of nearby hotels and the rates. When you make reservations, mention you are with the cat show. The club may have negotiated a special rate and you will have to mention your affiliation in order to get the rate. Even if the hotel rate is a standard one, the club may have set aside a block of rooms at a particular hotel for use by exhibitors. Having these rooms filled may help the club get the same hotel for its next show.

The general information section of a flyer provides you with other details necessary to the show. It gives the show hours (during which you must be present in the showhall), the scoring system and where you can get a copy of the sponsoring federation's show rules.

THE ENTRY FORM

Accompanying the show flyer will be an entry form and a summary sheet. You fill out both these forms, enclose your entry fee and mail all three to the Entry Clerk.

Some federations have adopted an official entry form that must be used when entering the show. Other federations permit the club sponsoring a show to use its own form. If you often enter the same cat in shows in federations using an official form (such as CFA or TICA), you can fill out a master form and just have it copied when you need it to enter a show. Remember to leave any places blank that change from show to show, such as "age at show."

Entry forms are usually self-explanatory. If you do have a problem with a form, call the Entry Clerk for help. The most common difficulty when you enter for the first time is filling in the section for your region. States are in different regions in different federations. Also, as the federations enlarge their memberships, they may move states from one region to another. If you don't know your region, just leave it blank. The Entry Clerk will have the latest regional map and can fill that in for you. If you guess your region and get it wrong, it may take extra time for your points to be confirmed.

Although they are not all the same, entry forms for all federations use many of the same terms and ask for similar information. Here are some terms you may encounter when entering a show:

Name of Cat: This is the official, registered name of the cat and not the name you call it ("Nekomo Caught in the Act of Jacat"—not "Kiri").

Reg. No.: Fill in the federation registration number here. If you have applied for the number, but don't have it yet, put "pending" here and tell the Entry Clerk the number as soon as you have it. Never fill in a registration number from another federation. *The registration number must be from the federation governing the show.*

Birth Date: This is the official birth date of the cat as taken from the registration form, and not the date you brought it home.

Sex: Male, Female, Alter or Spay.

Eye Color: This should be taken from the registration form.

Breed: The complete name should be used ("Japanese Bobtail"—not "JBT").

Color: This should also be taken from the registration form (such as "Black"), exactly the way it is *printed* there.

THE CAT FANCIERS' ASSOCIATION, INC.

OFFICIAL

ENTRY BLANK

It is the responsibility of the Exhibitor to enter his cat under its correct registered name, registered ownership, and in the correct class. Consult the CFA Registration Certificate for the **EXACT** registered name, registered ownership, and other data required for entry.

The Show Management is expressly **PROHIBITED** from accepting a Championship, Premiership, Provisional Breed or AOV entry unless the Entry Blank contains the registration number as shown on the registration certificate.

AVOID ERRORS - TYPE OR PRINT

NAME OF CAT

MO / DAY / YR

CFA REG. NO.   BIRTHDATE   SEX   EYE COLOR

BREED   COLOR   COLOR CLASS NUMBER

SIRE

DAM

BREEDER   AGENT

OWNER   PHONE: AREA CODE   NUMBER

STREET ADDRESS   CITY   STATE / PROVINCE   ZIP / POSTAL CODE

NAME OF SHOW   LOCATION OF SHOW   DATE OF SHOW

CIRCLE NUMBER OF REGION OF RESIDENCE (IF KNOWN)	1 NORTH ATLANTIC	2 NORTH WEST	3 GULF SHORE	4 GREAT LAKES	5 SOUTH WEST	6 MID WEST	7 SOUTHERN

I hereby enter the above named cat, at my own risk, subject to the provisions of the Show Rules of the Cat Fanciers' Association, Inc. in effect for this show, and I state that I am familiar with the provisions of these rules. (A copy of the current Show Rules may be obtained from the CFA Central Office, 1309 Allaire Ave. Ocean, NJ 07712. Price is $2.00)
I hereby state that the information provided on this Entry Blank is true and correct to the best of my knowledge.

SIGNATURE OF OWNER: _____
(If owner is under 18 yrs. of age, this blank must be signed by owner's parent or guardian.)

CAT TO BE ENTERED IN: (Check Proper Class and List Names of Shows)

NON-CHAMPIONSHIP	CHAMPIONSHIP	PREMIERSHIP	SPECIAL REQUESTS
☐ KITTEN	☐ OPEN	☐ OPEN	NON-SMOKING _____
☐ HOUSEHOLD PET	☐ CHAMPION	☐ PREMIER	(IF AVAILABLE)
☐ PROVISIONAL BREED	☐ GRAND CHAMPION	☐ GRAND PREMIER	DOUBLE CAGE _____
☐ _____ OTHER			SALES CAGE _____

BENCH WITH _____

Use the official CFA entry form when entering CFA shows.   © *1989 CFA.*

Color Class: This is the division in which the cat will be judged (such as "Solid"). You should find this out for each federation you show in, as it is not the same for all.

Sire: Use the complete name, including any of the appropriate designations earned by the cat, as given on the registration form ("NW, GC Nekomo Hirohito").

Dam: Use the complete name, including any appropriate federation designations earned by the cat, as given on the registration form ("GC Nekomo Kaede").

Breeder: Insert the name(s) of the breeders of the cat, and not the one who sold you the cat, if the two are different.

Agent: If you are having someone else take the cat to the show and show it the name of that person should go here.

Owner: This should be the name of the registered owner of the cat, or both names if the cat is owned jointly with someone else.

Phone/Address: The owner's phone and address.

Region: If you don't know, the Entry Clerk will determine your region from your address.

Signature: Even if the cat is owned by more than one person, only one signature is required.

Class—nonchampionship: Use this section when you are entering a cat that *cannot* earn titles for one reason or another.

Kitten: Under eight months of age.

Provisional Breed: These are breeds that have not yet been recognized for Championship titles.

NBC: A new breed or color that is being shown as a prerequisite to having the cat accepted for judging in the Championship class.

Classes/Championship: In these classes, cats can earn titles. This section is for purebred cats only.

    Open: A cat that has not fulfilled the requirements for the title of "Champion" in a given federation.

    Champion: A cat that is a "Champion" and is competing for the title of "Grand Champion."

    Grand Champion: A cat competing as a "Grand Champion."

Classes/Premiership: In these classes, all the male cats must be altered and all females must be spayed. This section is also for purebred cats only.

Open: An altered cat that has not fulfilled the requirements for the title of "Premier."

Premier: An altered cat that is a "Premier" and is competing for the title of "Grand Premier."

Grand Premier: An altered cat competing as a "Grand Premier."

Name of Show: This is the show you are entering.

For Sale: Place a check mark here if the cat you are entering is for sale.

Ex. Only: A cat that will be brought to the show and benched, but not judged. The abbreviation stands for "Exhibition Only."

Pedigreed Section: Fill in this section for all cats other than HHPs and HHP kittens.

Status: This designates the title your cat already holds. Circle the appropriate title.

- *Kitten*: No titles can be earned by kittens under eight months of age.
- *Novice*: An untitled cat competing for a TICA title.
- *Champion*: Champion.
- *Gr. Ch.*: Grand Champion.
- *Db. Gr. Ch.*: Double Grand Champion.
- *Tr. Gr. Ch.*: Triple Grand Champion.
- *Qd. Gr. Ch.*: Quadruple Grand Champion
- *Sp. Gr. Ch.*: Supreme Grand Champion.

Division: These are the color divisions in which cats of the same breed are judged. You may find the information on your registration form. Circle the appropriate color.

Household Pet Section: Use this section when entering an HHP. Note that CFA does not award *titles* to HHPs, although HHPs are judged at individual CFA shows.

Status: See the Pedigreed Section above. The titles are the same with the exception that the title "Master" is used in place of "Champion" when referring to HHPs.

Division: This is the color division in which your cat will be judged.

Eye Color: Take this information from the registration form.

Hair: This designates longhair or shorthair. If you're not sure, look at the length of the hair on the tail. If the cat has short hair but long hair on the tail, it is a longhair.

TICA
The International Cat Association
OFFICIAL ENTRY BLANK
Circle all applicable data

ALL CATS		
Region	**Sex**	**Catalog**
SW NW	Male	Kitten
SC NC	Neuter	Champ
SE NE	Female	Alter
JN CN	Spay	HHP Kit
UK		HHP
		NBC
Days		Ex. Only
Sat. Sun. Both		

PEDIGREE SECTION	
Status	**Division**
Kitten	Solid
Novice	Tortie
Champion	Tabby
Gr. Ch.	Shaded
Db. Gr. Ch.	Particolor
Tr. Gr. Ch.	Solid Point
Qd. Gr. Ch.	Lynx Point
Sp. Gr. Ch.	Tortie Point
	Particolor Point

HOUSEHOLD PET SECTION		
Status	**Division**	
Kitten	Solid	Solid & White
Senior	Tortie	Tortie & White
Master	Tabby	Tabby & White
Gr. Mstr.	Pointed	Pointed & White
Db. Gr. Mstr.	Shaded	Shaded & White
Tr. Gr. Mstr.		
Qd. Gr. Mstr.	**Hair**	
Sp. Gr. Mstr.	Longhair	Shorthair

NAME OF CAT: _____ BREED: _____

COLOR OF CAT: _____ EYE COLOR: _____

TICA REG. NO.: _____ AGE AT SHOW: _____ YRS. _____ MOS BIRTHDATE: _____

SIRE: _____ PRICE, IF FOR SALE: _____

DAM: _____ BENCHING: _____

BREEDER: _____ AGENT, IF ANY: _____

OWNER: _____
NAME _____ ADDRESS _____ PHONE

I hereby enter the above cat at my own risk, subject to the conditions in the Show Rules of THE
INTERNATIONAL CAT ASSOCIATION and agree to abide by the rulings of the Show Committee. _____
9-1-84   SIGNATURE

Use the official TICA entry form when entering TICA shows.   © 1989 TICA.

Cat's Name _____ Color _____ Sex

Registration No. _____ Breed _____ Eye Color _____ Birthdate

Sire's Name _____ Registration No. (if required)

Dam's Name _____ Registration No. (if required)

Breeder _____ Agent

Owner's Name

Owner's Complete Address

_____ Phone No.

Any questions pertaining to this entry will be phoned **COLLECT.**

It is the responsibility of the exhibitor to: (1) be sure that CFF registration can
be accomplished; (2) enter his cat under the correct registered name, registered
ownership and in the correct class. Consult CFF Registration Certificate for the
EXACT data required for entry.

*I certify that I am the actual owner of this cat (or duly appointed agent), and that I have
read the above and agree to abide by* **CFF** *rules.*

Signature of owner/agent

CHECK PROPER CLASS

NON-CHAMPIONSHIP
☐ Kitten
☐ AOV
☐ Experimental Breed

HOUSEHOLD PET
☐ Kitten ☐ LH ☐ SH
☐ Adult   ☐ LH ☐ SH

CHAMPIONSHIP
☐ Novice
☐ Champion
☐ Grand Champion
☐ Master Grand Champion

ALTERED DIVISION
☐ Novice
☐ Champion
☐ Grand Champion
☐ Master Grand Champion

SPECIAL BENCHING INSTRUCTIONS

PRICE IF FOR SALE

An entry form for use when entering a CFF show.   © 1989 CFF.

Benching: This area is for any special benching requests you might have (such as "bench with Vella/McGonagle").

THE SUMMARY SHEET

The summary sheet is an overview of *what* you pay for, with prices. This is used by the club to make life easier in processing your entry. If there is a summary sheet with your entry, fill it out completely and enclose it with your entry and fees. Be certain to type or print clearly.

Most summary sheets are self-explanatory. If you are entering for one day, or two days, early bird (if offered) or regular entry fee, put a check by the appropriate line. If you want a double cage, or to be benched at the end of a row, check the line. If you are taking out an advertisement in the catalog, check the size you want. Total the fees and options you will be paying for. Be sure to put your name, address and telephone number on the summary sheet. Sometimes, the benching request must also be put on the summary sheet.

SHOW ENTRY CONFIRMATION

Once you have entered a show, you will get a confirmation from the Entry Clerk. This lets you know your entry has been accepted and designates how your entry will be listed in the show catalog.

As soon as you get your show confirmation, check all the information for accuracy. While the confirmation does not follow a set form, the following information should be on it, in some order:
- Name of the show you have entered.
- Date(s) of the show you have entered.
- Cat's name.
- Cat's title, if any.
- Name of the sire.
- Name of the dam.
- Breeder's name.
- Owner's name.
- Registration number of the cat.
- Breed of the cat.
- Class in which your cat will be competing (status).
- Birth date of your cat or the age of the cat at the show, or both.
- Color or color division of the cat (such as "red solid") or both.

91

```
                    National Maine Coon Cat Club
                 Show Confirmation for 05/13-14/89
              Tony Laufnick - Entry Clerk  201-238-7892
                1 Oaktree Road - Sayreville, NJ  08872
                    Please Call Before 10pm
-------------------------------------------------------------------
John McGonagle                                          EXB # 37
                              PA   18103
Bench Request> Richbourg/Knopp
-------------------------------------------------------------------

Class> 6691 Other J B Colors Female JAPANESE BOBTAIL (Patterned Mi-Ke)
     NEKOMO CAUGHT IN THE ACT OF JACAT       Title> OPN
     Rn> 6691-489282     Dob> 07/07/88       Age> 0yr10mo
     Sr> GRC,NW Nekomo Mirohito
     Dm> GRC Nekomo Kaede
     Br> Allen Scruggs/Douglas Myers
     Ow> Carolyn Vella/John McGonagle  (1)

---------< Financial Summary by CompuShow,  Serial # 877621 >---------

   1 Regular Entry(s)..................... at $ 38.00 ea = $     38.00
   1 Extra Cage(s)....................... at $ 15.00 ea = $     15.00
-----------------------------------                    ---------
| Please notify the entry clerk    |   Sub-Total Due = $     53.00
| of any incorrect information     |   Total Rec'd   = $     53.00
| before closing date of 04/30/89  |                    ---------
-----------------------------------    Balance Due   = $       .00

****************************SHOW NOTES****************************************
*     Our show hotel is:      HOLIDAY INN AT                    *
*                             2117 ROUTE 4 EASTBOUND            *
*                                    NEW JERSEY 07024           *
*                                                               *
*                                                               *
*           BE SURE TO SAY YOU'RE WITH THE SHOW                 *
*                                                               *
*           CHECK-IN BEGINS 8AM ON SATURDAY                     *
*      Judging begins 10am Saturday and 9:30am on Sunday        *
****************************************************************************
                THANK YOU FOR ENTERING OUR SHOW!!!!!
```

You will receive a confirmation that your entry has been accepted into a show.

KEESTONE KATZ - SUMMARY SHEET

Name:_____FIRST SHOW? [] YES [] NO

ADDRESS: _____

CITY: _____ STATE: _____ ZIP: _____

PHONE: (home) _____ (work) _____

BENCHING REQUEST (one name only please): _____
****
EARLY BIRD (CLOSING DATE = FEBRUARY 28, 1989)

_____ 1 DAY ENTRIES @$25 -----------------------> $_____

_____ 2 DAY ENTRIES @$37 -----------------------> $_____

REGULAR (CLOSING DATE = APRIL 15, 1989)

_____ 1 DAY ENTRIES @$32 -----------------------> $_____

_____ 2 DAY ENTRIES @$48 -----------------------> $_____

_____ 3 - 2 DAY ENTRIES @$125 ------------------> $_____

_____ LISTING FEE @$5 each non-registered cat ---> $_____

_____ DOUBLE CAGE @$20 each --------------------> $_____

_____ CATALOG @3 each --------------------------> $_____

        *** SUBSTITUTIONS ARE $10 EACH (none after 4/15/89) ***

[] Full page ad @$25 ----------------------------> $_____

[] Half page ad @$15 ----------------------------> $_____

[] Business Card ad @$5 -------------------------> $_____

[] Donation to show general fund (Thank You) ----> $_____

TOTAL ===> $_____

TOTAL PAYMENT ENCLOSED >>>>>>>>>>>>>>>>>>>>>>>>>> $_____

Make all checks payable to: **KEESTONE KATZ**

MAIL ENTRY, SUMMARY SHEET AND PAYMENT TO:

HELEN C.

LANSDALE, PA 19446

CHECK HERE IF AVAILABLE TO CLERK: [] SATURDAY   [] SUNDAY

PLEASE NOTE: We will call collect if any questions arise
regarding your entries. A fee of $20 will be charged on all
checks returned for any reason.

A typical summary sheet for use when entering a show.

93

- Any additional requests for which you have paid (such as "double cage").
- Region in which you reside.

The confirmation form may carry additional information such as:

- Benching request.
- Acknowledgment of a donation made to the club.
- Whether you have prepaid for a show catalog.
- Eye color of the cat.

Since all the information on the show confirmation is important, correct it immediately if any mistake has been made. If you have time, you can correct it by letter to the Entry Clerk. But do it right away.

If you have received the confirmation just before the show, call the Entry Clerk and correct any errors over the telephone. Much of this information must go in the judges' books and the records the Master Clerk uses. If the information is wrong, it can cause a delay when you try to confirm an earned title with the federation's head office.

Some federations, such as TICA, have a rule that states how much time the Entry Clerk has to send out the confirmation. This information appears in the show rules of each federation. If it is past the date when you should have received the confirmation, call the Entry Clerk and check on the status of your entry. Unless the Entry Clerk is a professional service, this will be done by a member of the club sponsoring the show. Sometimes, show entries will be allowed to accumulate for a while before they are confirmed.

ONE-, TWO- AND THREE-DAY SHOWS

If you are exhibiting at a two-day or three-day show, you may or may not have to be present for the entire two or three days in order for your points to count. This depends upon the rules of the federation and on how the show was technically scheduled. In general the following can be used as a guide:

- *ACFA* permits shows to be scheduled either of two ways. First, a single show may cover an entire weekend. In that case, you must plan to exhibit for both days. Second, two shows may be held on a weekend—one show Saturday and an entirely new show Sunday. In this case, you can enter for either one day or both days.
- *CFA* usually runs just one show that covers both days of a week-

end. You are required to stay in the showhall for the two days in order to collect your points. Occasionally, a show will be held with all Champions and kittens judged on one day and all Premiers and HHPs judged on the other day. In this case, you are only benched for the day your cat will be judged.

- *CFF* uses the option of one show per day or one show each day with the sponsoring club making the decision which of the two to present.
- *TICA* usually offers one show each day. You can enter any or all of the shows. Occasionally, you will see a show at which Champions and kittens are judged on one day, with Alters and HHPs judged the other day. In that case, plan to be at the show only on the day your cat is being judged. TICA also has many shows that are held for three days, the third day usually being the Friday preceding the weekend. The show on Friday usually starts late in the afternoon and runs into the evening in order to accommodate exhibitors who want to exhibit all three days of the show.

You can determine how a show is being run by the information on the show flyer and entry form. If you have any questions, contact the Entry Clerk for assistance. Whether the show is one day or two days, you will usually have to stay until the end of the official show hours for your points to count.

Cat shows are advertised so that spectators may come to the show and appreciate the beautiful cats. Many spectators later become exhibitors themselves.

6

Now You Are
at the Show

TODAY, you will rarely find a cat show that is "vetted": that is, a show that requires a veterinarian to inspect each cat that comes into the showhall before judging begins. Most of today's shows are nonvetted for reasons of practicality. With so many cats being shown today, the amount of time "vetting" takes is unacceptable to exhibitors and show officials alike. It can also cause a great deal of stress for the cat, which may have to be kept in a carrier for an indefinite period of time. In addition, many cat show exhibitors are professionals. Whether they are running breeding catteries or showing neutered household pets, no responsible cat owners will risk bringing a sick cat to a show and no responsible show committee would allow this to happen.

If the show you choose will be vetted, it will specifically say so on the show flyer. The veterinary check is usually handled either before benching or after benching and before judging.

If one of your cats fails the vet check, leave the show with the cat that failed, any other cats you may have brought to show, even if they passed the vet check, and all your equipment. If you were scheduled to show different cats the second day, but one of your cats failed the vet check the first day, you usually will not be allowed to bring the other cats into the showhall the next day.

The veterinarian in a vetted show checks for signs of infectious diseases or other contagious problems, such as ringworm. He or she may also check your shot records, particularly if you will be showing a cat in a state or country that requires cats to have a rabies vaccination. So,

Most cat shows have a theme. The theme for the show sponsored by the National Exotic Shorthair Breed Club and the Scottish Fold Fanciers (CFF clubs) was "Hawaiian Cruise." The gifts given to the winners in the rings were from Hawaii and the show decor was bright and colorful.

When you get to the showhall, immediately go to the area designated for checking in to the show. At check-in you will be told where you will be benched. This is also where you get your catalog of the show.

if you are going to a vetted show, make sure you have a complete shot record for all of your cats with you.

Regardless of whether the examination is done before you enter the hall or before your cat is judged, you will have to complete the check-in procedure we describe in the next section.

CHECK-IN PROCEDURE

The nonvetted show, one in which your cat need not be checked by a vet before it can be shown, is the rule in the United States. As with the vetted show, you should be able to find a notation on the flyer for the show that the show is nonvetted.

Either on your show flyer or in the confirmation is information on when you can check in at the show. As you enter the showhall, you will find a table where you will be checking in. Give your name to the show officials and they will give you any paperwork required for entering the showhall and provide you with your cat's entry number. You will have received a confirmation form from the Entry Clerk, which you should have with you in case there are any questions or problems.

Once you are checked in, you will be directed to the area where you will be benched. You will be given a catalog if you have paid for it in advance or if it is included in your entry fee. If the catalog is sold separately, this is when you should buy it.

In some two-day shows, you will also be required to check in the second day even though you may be showing the same cats. At that time, you only have to tell the Entry Clerk the number your cat has been assigned for the show. If check-in is required after the first day, do it. If you do not, your cat is marked absent and will not be called to the rings for judging.

If you arrive late—that is, after the posted hours for checking in— you must still check in. In this case, once you are finished at the Entry Clerk's desk, you also will be directed to go to *every* ring clerk and tell them that you and your cat are now present in the showhall. This is the only way to remove yourself from the list of those who are absent. Usually the best way to do this is to write your cat's number on a slip of paper with the word "present" and leave it with the ring clerks after you have told them you are present.

Ardee Ashlea, a Black Smoke Devon Rex kitten bred and owned by Rosaline Dolak De Dan, looks around in wonder at her first show.

The exhibitors transform the showhall into a place of excitement.

YOUR CAGE

In preparing for the show, you will have to prepare for the care and comfort of your cat and yourself. If you are attending a show for just one day, this is fairly easy. If you will be staying at the show hotel, you will need additional equipment for both you and your cat. All the equipment you bring into the showhall, with the exception of a grooming table, must fit in, on or under your benching area, leaving room for a chair and you.

The benching cages are made of wire on the top and all sides, but with an open bottom set on plastic-covered wooden tables. If you request and pay for a "double cage," you will get the cage measuring twenty-two by twenty-two by forty-four inches. The size of the cages can vary slightly and is generally noted in the show flyer. All cats entered in the show and all kittens brought to the show for sale must be kept in these cages. Most federations do not permit cats or kittens to be kept in carrier cages in the showhall. Most clubs, and some federations, will specify how many cats or kittens (or both) can be kept in a single benching cage. You must always abide by these rules or risk being disqualified by the sponsoring club or even by the sanctioning federation itself.

If you are showing a large cat, your cat might be more comfortable in a double cage. The single cage can be much too cramped for a cat the size of a Maine Coon or a Ragdoll.

Cleaning the Cage

Before you set up the cage, you should clean and disinfect it and the surrounding area. The easiest way to disinfect the cage is to use an aerosol or spray preparation made to disinfect veterinary examination tables. These preparations are available through professional animal-grooming supply catalogs, or through your veterinarian. Some exhibitors simply bring a sponge saturated in disinfectant or diluted chlorine bleach, then sealed in a plastic bag.

Setting Up the Benching Cage

After you have disinfected the cage, lift the cage and cover the bottom of the wooden platform. This enables you to spread the required cage bottom covering smoothly and easily. However, you must be careful when lifting the cage off the platform. The cages are meant to collapse and they tend to do so as soon as they are removed from the platform.

The benching cage opens completely at the top.

A benching cage can be set up using a pillow-case attached to the cage with alligator clips.

The benching cage itself may be removed in order to cover the floor of the cage.

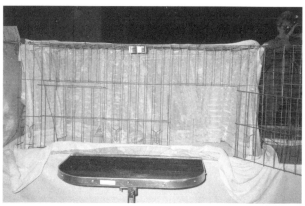

A grooming table provides a comfortable footing for the cat during grooming.

Be careful putting the cage back. The cage has to fit inside the raised wooden strips on the platform, or it may fall to the floor.

If you are using a single cage, remember that the other half of it is your benching neighbor's cage. Be careful not to disturb your neighbor's cage setup when you are setting up your own cage. Do not lift your cage off the platform after your neighbor has set up. Also, don't put your floor covering under the divider and into your neighbor's cage.

Cage Curtains

Once the cage has a floor covering in place, attach curtains to the back and the sides of the cage using the inside walls. As an exhibitor, you are *required* to cover your benching cage, usually on the sides and bottom. The reason for this is not cosmetic; it is protective. Cats become curious and try to paw around to the next cage in an effort to get to know their neighbor. If you have a female in heat, she may be looking for a mate. If you are benched next to a whole male who sprays, you want to protect your cat from any spray that may have saturated the male cat's cage curtains.

Ideally, you should bring coverings not only for the sides and bottom of the cage, but also for the top. These coverings, usually called "cage curtains," can be as simple or as elaborate as you desire, but it should be possible to wash all materials used for cage curtains in hot water and disinfectant frequently.

Most experienced exhibitors use a double set of cage curtains or other liners to provide extra warmth for their cat. In the winter, some showhalls can be drafty, and the double lining can keep your cat more comfortable.

The nondecorative cage liner can be something as simple as a piece of plastic sheeting, a felt-lined plastic tablecloth or even a plastic garbage bag attached tautly to the sides of the cage. The inner, usually more decorative, cage curtains can be real curtains on curtain rods attached by twist ties to the top of the cage. They can also be sheeting or towels or pillowcases attached to the cage by alligator clips or clothespins. Some exhibitors buy or sew a one-piece cage curtain setup.

Securing the Benching Cage

Close the top of the cage if you previously opened it. Usually you have to make sure that the top catches at each corner and that the hooks built in to the top along the edges are caught under the top edge of the cage walls. Some of the cages used by various clubs are older and may not close satisfactorily. For this reason, you may want to bring some twist ties to the show. These are very helpful in keeping the top of the cage secure.

Even though it is not always required to cover the top of the cage, it is a good idea to do so. You may be keeping show supplies on top of the cage and these supplies can spill. So you will want to make sure that any spilled liquid cannot run down into your cage and all over your cat. Some exhibitors will use a hard plastic tray, plastic bin or plastic litter box on top of the cage to hold any liquid items and provide a hard surface, whether or not they also cover the top of the cage.

At some shows, you will see exhibitors using a lock on the benching cage. This is to prevent spectators from opening the door of the cage. Some spectators honestly are not aware that they are not to open the cage. Others feel that if a "For Sale" sign is on the cage, they are free to open the cage door to look at the kittens. If you are in a large showhall, the show is crowded and you and those you are benched with are at the judging ring, your unattended cage can be an invitation to trouble. A lock will at least keep people from opening the door. Fortunately, most spectators don't know that the benching cage is not secured to the base of the platform, so they don't try to lift it off.

GROOMING AT THE SHOW

Of course, most grooming has already been done before the show, but you may still want to do some grooming, just to touch up your cat, at the show itself. Since you want your cat to look its best for each and every judge, groom the cat before taking it to the ring.

The supplies you bring will vary according to how much grooming you do and the hair length of the cat you are showing. Include brushes, combs, cornstarch baby powder and any specialized cleaners you use, such as those used around the eye.

You should also bring some extra supplies that you might need in an emergency. Some cats get diarrhea at the show and will need to be cleaned. In the judging ring, your cat may be caged next to a male cat who sprays while waiting to be judged. If this happens, you will need to clean your cat at the show.

You may want to use a grooming table for your cats' comfort while being groomed at the show, especially if they are used to being groomed this way at home. There are several different types of grooming tables:

- Four-legged grooming tables, with rubber surfaces, which collapse and can be taken easily to cat shows.

Supreme Grand Champion Maineline's Augustus of Donnahugh ("Augie") is groomed before judging by his owner, Donna Richbourg.

Once you have your cage set up, find where the litter and portable litter boxes are provided.

- Semicircular grooming tables, which connect to the wooden benching table and stand on one adjustable leg. This is a good table for a small cat or a cat that does not require much grooming at the show.
- A setup that consists of a carpeted platform with casters and another carpeted platform with connecting elastic ropes. You use this by placing the castered platform on the floor, putting your travel cage on that platform and topping it with the other platform. The two platforms are held together with the elastic rope. This system can accommodate one or two travel cages and has the advantage of providing both a wheeled travel cage and a built-in grooming surface. During the show, you can store extra supplies in the empty travel cages.
- A television tray table topped with a towel can also serve as an excellent, lightweight yet inexpensive grooming surface.

SUPPLIES AND EQUIPMENT

For some, the best way to handle the cat care items is to have a "Mommy Bag" or a "Person Bag." It was called a "Mommy Bag" because the custom used to be to call all cat owners "Mommy," even if they were men. Now, we call it a "Person Bag." In that bag you keep all the supplies you need for your cat, separating them from what you bring for yourself. The supplies for cats and people combined make a wheeled luggage cart or dolly an essential item for the cat show exhibitor.

Cat Supplies Checklist
- Food dish (if not provided or if desired)
- Litter box (if not provided or if desired)
- Water dish (if not provided or if desired)
- Bed (if desired)
- Toy(s)
- Cloth for bottom of cage
- Cage curtains for sides of cage
- Top cover for cage
- Tray or bin (for holding supplies on top of the cage)
- Clothespins, alligator clips, twist ties (for setting up curtains and securing the cage)
- Cage locks (if desired)
- Disinfectant (for cage and for disinfecting your hands)

Supreme Grand Champion Godivasweets Golden Girl is "polished" by her owner, Carol Decker White, before being judged.

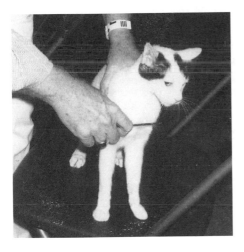

GRC Nekomo Akambo (Baby) is used to cat shows. She was the Seventh-Best Kitten Nationally in CFA for the show year 1988–1989.

One vendor sells custom-made cat trees at shows.

Cat show vendors carry a large selection of supplies and toys at excellent prices.

Vendors sell many types and sizes of travel cages and cat beds at shows and have the lowest prices on supplies.

Kent Wallace decorates pumpkins with cat faces at a show held just before Halloween. Kent is also a caricaturist.

Photographers who specialize in taking pictures of cats are found at many cat shows.

- Grooming brushes and combs
- Chamois cloth (shorthair cats)
- Nail scissors
- Trimming scissors
- Cornstarch baby powder (for grooming longhair cats, eliminating oil on cats' coats, and keeping your hands dry)
- Coat gloss
- Eye cleaning preparations
- Instant or dry shampoo (for emergencies)
- Paper towels
- Baby wipes (for cleaning hands and, in an emergency, spot cleaning the cat)
- Diarrhea medication (if your cat is prone to developing diarrhea, it will do so at a show)
- Cat treats
- Special cat food (if desired or not provided)
- Plastic trash bag
- Cotton balls
- Cotton swabs
- Alcohol

Exhibitor Supplies

While the main focus is on your cat, you must also provide for yourself. You will be spending anywhere from six to ten hours in the showhall each day. In addition, you have travel time, as well as time grooming your cat the day of the show. Needless to say, you need to provide for your own comfort, as well as the cat's.

People Food

Most clubs that sponsor shows make certain that food for people is available in the showhall itself. If that is not possible, and sometimes it is not, the club usually will let you know what food is available in the area near the showhall.

Although the individual rings at the show will break for lunch, they don't usually break at the same time, so there may not be a designated "lunch hour" during the show itself during which you can expect to be able to slip away for lunch. You will have to decide the best time to get lunch in between judgings of your cat. If you are showing more than one cat, especially if they are in different categories, divisions or classes,

Many shows hold raffles to help defray the cost of the show or to start the funding for the club's next show. The raffle prizes, usually donated by club members or vendors, are plentiful and sometimes of exceptional quality. Winning a raffle prize is an added surprise in any show.

You will find many cats and kittens for sale or adoption at a cat show.

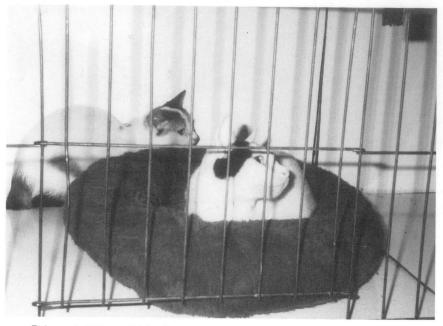

Baby and a kitten watching the spectators from the comfort of a benching cage.

In this showhall, the spectators could look down into a judging ring.

your time may be limited. For these reasons, many exhibitors bring their own lunch.

Cash

You will need some cash for the catalog and vending machines. Also, many cat clubs hold raffles at the shows to raise money for a new club just starting up or to help defray the costs of putting on a show. Sometimes a nonkill animal shelter will be represented at a show and may hold a raffle to raise money for the shelter. If you are interested in participating in any or all of these raffles, and this is not required, bring some cash for raffle tickets.

Cat shows are the best places for buying your supplies as well. Many vendors are represented at the shows and they carry everything from litter boxes and grooming supplies to collectible ceramic statues. The prices at the shows are very reasonable. In many cases, they are actually less than you would spend for supplies purchased through a catalog of professional animal supplies. Also, most vendors will gladly accept a check from an exhibitor. Some, but not all, accept credit cards as well.

THE TOTAL LEARNING EXPERIENCE

From time to time, you will find that the show's sponsors have arranged some events to be held just before, during or immediately after the show. Clubs arrange these for a variety of reasons: to make their show different from others; to accommodate the federation's needs for additional training of judges or clerks; to honor the outstanding cats of the previous season or to encourage exhibitors to come to the show for an extra day. It can be said that there is something for everyone in events that range from educational to social.

- *Breed seminar*: You will see a presentation on one or more breeds of cats, outlining their history, their genetics, and what points a judge looks for in the ring.
- *Genetics or health seminar*: An expert will talk about cat genetics or health, usually focusing on a particular problem or issue such as Feline Leukemia Virus. The expert is also usually willing to answer questions on a broader range of topics.
- *Cat care seminar*: This usually covers grooming and presenting cats, although related issues of health and nutrition will also usually be covered.

- *Clerking school*: This is one of the steps required of all people who wish to become Licensed Clerks. Some people will attend a clerking school to just learn, in more detail, how a ring operates and the mechanics of keeping score at a show.
- *Judging school or refresher session*: These meetings cover the mechanics of judging, sometimes focusing on changes in show rules or in breed standards. Many, but not all of them, are open to nonjudges.
- *Judges' dinner*: This is a strictly social event, sponsored by the club, where you can meet club members and judges in a social environment. They range from very informal to somewhat formal.
- *Awards dinner*: These are often formal events, honoring the best cats of the previous show season. They are held at the regional and national level. If you have shown your cat actively in a federation during the show season, it can be entertaining to see competitors honored. It is a lot of fun if *your* cat is one of those honored.

Unless a session has a commercial sponsor, each of these may carry with it an additional fee and require you to make reservations in advance. If you are interested in any of these, contact the Show Manager for additional details. Most are open to any exhibitor, and they can be entertaining and educational.

7

Showhall Courtesy

ALTHOUGH A CAT SHOW is competitive, it can be a friendly place. Even if you don't socialize with other exhibitors outside the showhall, you will be spending six to ten hours of your day with them during a show. Shows are crowded and have their hectic times and their dull periods. Cats can be unpredictable. They decide to use the litterbox just as they are being called to the show ring. They may make a run for freedom when the cage door is opened. Even the most seasoned cat show exhibitors can forget to bring everything they need to the show.

As you can see, exhibitors need each other. For all these reasons, cat federations have developed specific rules governing the way cat shows are to be run, and exhibitors, cat clubs and show personnel have developed unofficial but definite standards of acceptable behavior.

Cat federation sanctioned shows should not be confused with local pet shows. Cat show exhibitors are professionals. The points and titles earned by cats being exhibited are crucial to the success of a cattery. This also holds true for HHP exhibitors, since HHPs are titled by most federations and recognized at the end of the season in a manner similar to that for purebred cats. To become a part of the cat show community, no matter what kind of cat you are showing, you must also have a professional attitude toward the show.

CFF Household Pet of the Year (1987–1988 and 1988–1989) Savoir Faire of Arubacat was CFF's first Master Grand Champion.

Ta-Raja Queen Ann's Lace, a Seal Point Siamese kitten, and CH Chanthara's Guinivere, a Blue Point Siamese cat, relax at the show between judging rings.

Master Grand Champion Te-mek's Sitamon was CFF's Cat of the Year (1988–1989). Sitamon, an Egyptian Mau, is a beautiful spotted cat. CFF gave the breed its first official recognition.

If you look at the perches in the show cage, you will see l'chi and Honeybear resting. They are both Birmans, a breed characterized by the distinctive white gloves on the paws.

DRESS

While there is no dress code for the showhall, there are a few simple guidelines. Since shows are held in different kinds of places, the specific site of the show should be considered when you dress. For example, a show held in a school auditorium may be much more casual than a show held in a major hotel's ballroom. A show held in a major convention center can bring in thousands of people as spectators. While you are there to gain points toward titles and even national awards, you also want to present a good image of the cat fancy to the spectators.

You will be sitting, standing and carrying your cat to the judging rings. You will also be doing some last-minute grooming of your cat before it is presented in the judging ring. For this reason, comfortable, washable sports clothes are usually worn by most exhibitors. Since show-halls tend to be overheated and crowded, you might wish take this into account when you dress. Comfortable shoes are a must.

BENCHING

Your benching—that is, exactly where in the showhall your cat is to be caged—has already been determined by the show management before you arrive at the hall. Their placements should reflect the number of cats you have entered as well as any special benching arrangements you have requested and paid for, such as end-of-row benching or a double cage for one entry. If you find your benching is not what you paid for with your entry, contact the show manager immediately—*before* you set up your cage. Never take it upon yourself to change your cage because you don't like it or because it is not what you paid for. That must be done by the show management.

If you filled in a benching request—that is, a request to be placed next to or near someone else who will be at the show—the show management usually tries to accommodate it. However, if the person you requested to bench with did not enter the show, or if many people requested benching next to a particular person, you may not get your benching request. This is generally not a reason to complain unless the person with whom you requested benching is to act as your agent for part of the show. If this is the case, again contact the show management at once.

Some shows bench cats by breed, so if you requested benching with someone who is showing a cat of a breed different from yours, you may not be benched with that person.

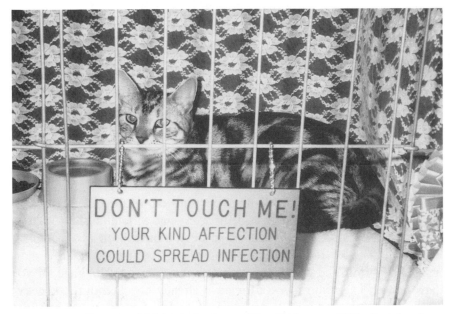

Master Grand Champion Midnight's Smokey, a Silver Tabby, was CFF's Best American Shorthair (1988–1989) and also the Ninth-Best Alter (1988–1989). The American Shorthair is a strong and hardy breed of cat.

This cage of British Shorthair cats consists of Bellerose's Prince Andrew and his littermates.

You can call the Entry Clerk about your benching request when you enter the show. However, most Entry Clerks do not do the benching. The most the Entry Clerk may be able to do is pass your request on to the person who will be doing the benching or put you in direct contact with that person.

The area you have been given in benching is the area you have to live in for the duration of the cat show. If you are only showing one cat and have paid for only cage space for that one entry, you will be "living" in an area only about twenty-two inches wide for the entire show. If this is the case, it may be rude to bring another person, a large grooming table and a lot of equipment.

To give yourself room so that you don't crowd the other exhibitors unnecessarily, you should consider purchasing a double cage for one entry. Regardless of the amount of space you have been assigned, it is usually best to keep any articles that will not be needed for the show itself away from the cage area. Items such as personal luggage, if you have not checked into a hotel (or have already checked out), or heavy coats (if you show during the winter), should be kept in your car.

After you have set up your cage, put any extra items under the stand supporting the benching cages and out of the way. Be careful, since the stands are often lightweight and easily moved by accident. Since the aisles between the cages will become crowded as the spectators arrive, keep your chair and your grooming table as close to the cage as possible.

Clean up any trash as soon as possible. Some shows even request that you clean the litterbox immediately after your cat defecates to help eliminate odor in the hall. Always put trash, including cat litter, in the receptacles located throughout the showhall.

Smoking may be permitted at some shows. If so, never smoke when you are at the judging ring or while grooming or carrying a cat. Smoke only in your own benching area (if allowed) unless you are visiting a cage where that exhibitor also smokes. If the person you are benched next to is not at the cage when his or her cat is called to a ring, try to find that person and report the call. Sometimes the loudspeaker systems can be difficult to hear throughout a hall, so if you are away from your cage, you may miss a ring call. However, never take anyone's cat up to the judging ring unless you have been specifically asked to do so by the owner.

HANDLING CATS

It is wonderful to admire other exhibitors' cats, and you can learn a lot about the various breeds from doing that. However, *never* touch anyone's cat without permission. Some cats are temperamental, or shy, and may bite a stranger. A cat may have just been groomed, so that handling it may make it necessary for the owner to regroom it.

Cats that are shown often become just like people who exhibit often. They develop their own routine for the shows. While they may appear to sleep, eat and use the box just as they do at home, these cats may not like to be disturbed. Remember, for the cats, a show is a different environment, and often a very strange one.

Many times, spectators fail to realize that the day before the show, the cat was bathed and groomed. The day of the show, the cat spent a lot of time in a travel cage in a car (or plane) and will spend several hours in a small benching cage. There will be grooming again before each judging ring and handling and examination by four to six different judges. The cat may be spending the night in a hotel room, away from the normal environment and the cats it lives with and plays with at home. A jar of baby food may be the only treat the cat has all weekend. That does not make it spoiled—just especially loved.

RING CALLS

Although most ring clerks give a first, second and eventually a third and final ring call, always try to bring your cat to the judging ring the first time your cat is called. If you do not do this, the judging in that ring may be delayed. Since a judge may handle an average of two hundred cats per day, even a slight delay in the flow of the judging ring can result in that ring running late. When one ring runs late, the entire show can run late.

If your cat is being judged or is in Finals in one ring and is called for judging in another, you have to inform the clerk for the ring in which you have just been called that your cat is in another ring. The clerk will take care of informing the judge, and you will have done all you can to avoid causing a delay.

THE JUDGING RING

There are times when you may want to or have to pull your cat out of a particular judging ring. Cats are pulled from rings for many reasons. For example, your cat may have become too nervous to be handled, so you let it rest for a while and calm down. Or your cat may have had a messy bowel movement and must be cleaned at the very moment it is

The judging ring is quiet before the show.

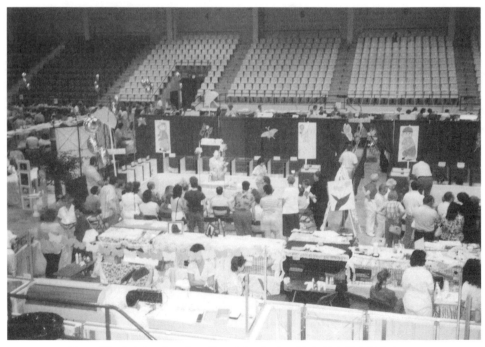

Two of the judging rings in action at the Garden State Cat Club (NJ) show.

due for judging. A cat should never be pulled from the judging ring just because the judge has never put your cat in the Finals. This is very unsportsmanlike, and a truly professional exhibitor would never do this. As a matter of fact, doing this can actually hurt other exhibitors. For example, in TICA you must have twenty-five cats judged in order for a Specialty ring to have the top ten in a Final. Fewer than twenty-five cats permits only the top five Finalists to receive bonus points. If pulling your cat reduces the number of cats being judged below twenty-five, you may deprive five exhibitors of valuable points.

If you must pull your cat from a particular ring, tell the clerk in that ring as soon as possible that you are removing your cat from that ring only. If you cannot get to the ring, you can ask another exhibitor going to the ring to tell the clerk, and most will do that. Your cat will be marked absent in that ring by the clerk.

The Judging Cage

Once you have caged your cat in the judging ring, you should not go back to the judging cage until the cat is released after it has been judged and scored. However, you should try to stay *at* the judging ring the entire time. Kittens, particularly, can get into all kinds of trouble despite the fact that the cage is empty except for them. They will play with the number on the top of the cage, trying to drag it inside the cage, they will try to "visit" the cat in the next cage, they will try to climb the cage, and they may even try to "escape" (which they sometimes can actually do). Since the judge and the clerk are busy, they cannot always keep an eye on your cat. You must watch your cat at all times.

Occasionally, your cat may urinate in the cage, or a male cat may spray. In that case, you will have to remove your cat from the cage while the cage is being recleaned. Some federations expect you to clean the cage yourself if this kind of accident occurs. Since it is not a rare occurrence, don't be embarrassed. Just try to be cooperative and clean up after your cat.

During Judging

Sometimes a judge will ask the owner of a particular cat to come up and remove the cat from its cage for judging. This generally means that the judge believes that he or she is unable safely to remove the cat for judging. If you are not there to help the judge, the cat may not be judged at all. If the judge calls for the owner of a cat to come up during or immediately after judging, that owner should do so at once. The reasons for this call may vary from a simple question about the color description of the cat in the judge's book ("Isn't this blue a blue cream?") to a suggestion ("This cat is very nervous: Perhaps it should be withheld from the next ring to settle down") to a warning ("This cat does not appear to be clean, and if I see it again in this condition, I will disqualify it"). Come up to the judge so that the conversation can be conducted in private.

After Judging

When your cat is ready to be returned to your cage after judging, remove it as quickly as possible from the ring. The judge or clerk will indicate this in one of two ways: Either the cat's number will be placed facedown or removed entirely from the judging cage, or the clerk or judge will announce that one or a group of cats "may go back" or "are released." When you take the cat out, leave the door open so that the steward knows to clean the cage. A good way to take your cat out of the cage is the way most judges do: Turn the cat's face toward the back of the cage and remove the cat with its back toward you.

Leave the ring quickly, avoiding getting in the way of the judge or other exhibitors. Do not let your cat stay in the judging cage after it has been released. This holds up the entire show.

Finals

When Finals are posted, get your cat to the ring as quickly as possible. A cat called for Finals that does not appear can be replaced by another cat, losing its points and awards. If your cat is being judged in another ring, go to the ring where it is being Finaled and tell the clerk, not the judge. Usually, the clerk will tell you to bring the cat over as soon as it is judged. Unless the two judges agree otherwise, judging takes priority over Finals in some federations.

It can be more difficult to be a good winner than it can be to be a good loser. Screaming when you win certainly keeps you from looking like a professional. It is also professional courtesy to congratulate all the winners, including the owners of the cats that placed higher than your cat did.

Many exhibitors ask judges to sign rosettes they have awarded to their cats. The proper time to do this is when you are picking up your cat after the judge has awarded all the Finals. As a general rule, this is not an appropriate time to ask the judge to critique your cat or to discuss

ACFA rosettes and Merit ribbons.

Sometimes your cat wins more than just a rosette when it Finals; it can win prizes too.

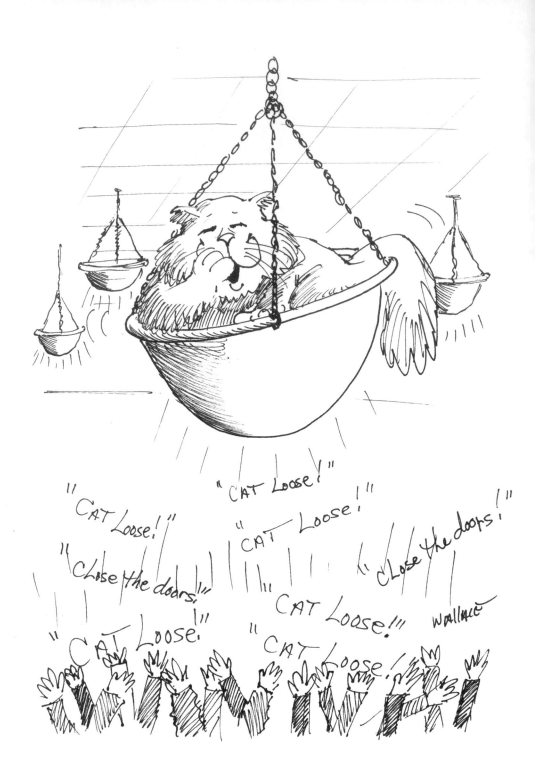

other matters with a judge. A simple "thank you" is sufficient. Conduct any other business with a judge at the end of the day, so that you do not delay other exhibitors.

SPECIAL ANNOUNCEMENTS

From time to time, an exhibitor may be called to a particular ring or to the master clerk's desk. The call is usually in the form "Will the owner of cat number 123 please come to ring 4." That means you, but *not* your cat. The reason for such a call is usually technical. You may have forgotten to pick up your rosette; the judge may have overlooked presenting a breed award to which your cat is entitled; there may be a question about your cat's color classification or age that must be cleared up. Regardless of the reason, answer a call promptly, which usually means listening very carefully to announcements, even when the showhall is crowded and very noisy.

A "*cat loose*" announcement is heard occasionally during the transfer of a cat from the carrying cage to the benching or judging cage. If the cat decides to take a brief run to show his owner who's boss, a cat may get loose from his owner or from a judge. When this happens, the cat generally makes a wild dash around the showhall. When a cat gets loose, you will hear the exhibitors shout "cat loose." This is a *very serious* situation and should be treated as such. If you are by a door leading to the outside of the showhall, and that door is open, shut it *immediately*. Never try to run after a loose cat, but if it comes your way let the owner know by calling out. The cat will eventually find a place to hide and will settle down and permit its owner to pick it up again.

If your cat gets loose, call out "cat loose" and try to follow your cat. Don't be upset. This happens all the time, even to the most seasoned exhibitors.

THE SPECTATORS

As cat shows have become more popular, the number of spectators has increased to the point that the sheer size of the gate has begun to cause some problems in the showhall. If the hall is too noisy, exhibitors may not be able to hear the ring call.

Despite this, a big gate is considered desirable. The spectators are, in many cases, potential exhibitors. Many people come to cat shows to buy kittens, so the breeders who are selling kittens appreciate a big gate. The gate receipts help to fund the sponsoring cat club and, indirectly, the next cat show that club sponsors. If one or more humane societies are represented at the show, they can expect donations from the gate. In many cases, these humane societies can place many of their cats for adoption because they are at the show. Vendors, both those who deal primarily with the professional exhibitor or breeder and those who have more general cat-related items, depend on the gate for sales. For many clubs, therefore, the benefits of a large gate far exceed the problems it can cause.

The following are some general rules for dealing with spectators.

1. Protect your cat. Remember that spectators do not know to disinfect before they touch your cat. You also don't know what animals they may have at home, or the condition of their animals. If, after spending some time talking to someone, you feel that there would not be a problem if that person touched your cat, do not hesitate to ask him or her to disinfect before and after touching your cat. Unless your cat is extremely docile, never let anyone pick up your cat. Your cat is under enough stress as it is without having someone hold it in a way it is not used to.

Many people keep signs on their cages telling the spectators not to touch the cats. These can be made at home or purchased from the vendors at the shows. These signs generally say "hands off" in a very cute way so they get the point across without being offensive. One sign we use says "Please Don't Pet Me—Even if I Ask!" Never hesitate to tell a spectator not to touch your cat. This not only protects the cat, it protects you.

Be especially careful of children. All the above suggestions hold true, but even more so. Unfortunately, sometimes children are left to run around the showhall without their parents. They don't know the rules and they must be told how to be careful in order to protect the cats and themselves. Children love to pet the cats, and they don't realize that they can cause a problem or that they may be hurt by a cat.

2. Protect your valuables. Always put purses and other valuables out of sight. They are easily stored in the cage you use to transport your cats. Store all your items under the benching cages. You can keep the grooming supplies on top of the cage if you put a firm cover over it first. Anything small and valuable can be put in the cage with the cat, especially if it can be hidden under a cat bed.

3. *Protect your neighbors*. During judging, you will often be away from your cage, as will your neighbors. For this reason, cat show exhibitors watch out for each other.

4. *Keep your chair as close to the cage as possible*. By keeping your chair as close to the cage as you can, you help keep the aisles as wide as possible. This enables the traffic to flow smoothly.

5. *Be friendly*. Most spectators are a delight. They will admire your cat and want to know all about it. You are also able to explain your breed to someone who may not know about the breed. If you are showing an HHP, you may help someone realize how special HHPs can be. You can do a great deal of good. Spectators like to tell you about their cats and you can tell them the importance of neutering and keeping a cat indoors. Many spectators want to become exhibitors and you can encourage them. There are spectators we have talked to at one show and benched next to a few shows later.

When you are a spectator, if exhibitors permit you to touch their cats, do not be insulted if they ask you to disinfect your hands first. This is not a reflection on how healthy your cat seems. Rather, it is an effort to protect their cat and the other cats they may have at home. After you handle someone else's cat, you may want to disinfect your hands before you handle your own cat. The goal here is more to keep the cats from getting sick from human contact than to keep them from getting sick from each other. Remember, every time a judge handles a cat, he or she must clean both the judging area and his or her hands.

We keep a dilute solution of Nolvasan, a commercial disinfectant, in a spray bottle on our cage just for this purpose. Just spray the disinfectant on your hands, rub your hands together and dry them with a paper towel. By doing this, you are helping to protect your cat's health.

Every exhibitor eventually returns to being a spectator. Maybe you are attending a show of a different federation to see how its shows are run before you enter one, maybe you are picking up a kitten or seeing a cat that may fit into your breeding program or maybe you are just visiting friends. Whatever the reason, you are now a spectator, no longer an exhibitor, and should act the way you want other spectators to act.

8

The Judging Day

$\mathbf{Y}$OU HAVE CHECKED in and benched your perfectly groomed cat in the disinfected, curtained benching cage, and you are ready for the show to begin.

The most important thing to remember is the entry number your cat was assigned. Your cat will be called by this number all day throughout the show. The entry number will be on a card on the cage, or given to you when you check in.

SHOW OFFICIALS

Several show officials are essential to making the judging day run as efficiently as possible.

The head ring clerk manages the ring and keeps track of how the judge scored the cats. If you are going to remove your cat from a particular ring, you will tell the ring clerk for that ring.

The ring steward cleans and disinfects the cages after a cat has been judged and released from the judging ring. The ring steward is not allowed to touch the cats benched in the judging ring.

The master clerk will keep track of the scores of *all* the cats judged during the show. The records will show which cat in each class scored the most points and has earned the honor as Best Cat in the show. These records also go to the national office of the show-sponsoring federation, and are the basis on which your cat will be awarded titles, and even regional and national recognition.

The judge will handle your cat and evaluate it according to the Standards of Perfection as formulated and adopted by the federation sanctioning the cat show. He or she will make the awards in the ring and determine the final top five or top ten cats in each class.

The show committee is a group of members of the club sponsoring the show. Typically, the show committee includes people such as the Entry Clerk, the show manager and other club members. They are responsible for keeping the show running smoothly. If you have a problem with how the show is run, contact the show committee at once.

THE SHOW CATALOG

The show catalog is a book printed for each show. It must contain certain items specified in the rules of the sanctioning federation. Once these items are accounted for, however, the catalog can be as plain or as lavish as the club chooses to make it. Some show catalogs are not only informative, they are works of art.

The show catalog usually contains the following items (the items marked with an asterisk are especially important to you):

1. The name and dates of the show.*
2. A list of judges.
3. The names of the head ring clerks.
4. Information about the club sponsoring the show.
5. Information concerning any special awards that are to be given at the show.
6. Any special information of interest to exhibitors, such as the location of a first-aid station.*
7. Any special information of interest to spectators.
8. Vendor and corporate advertisements.
9. Advertisements by breeders.
10. Information about the sponsoring federation.
11. Official federation forms for registration, membership, claiming of wins and keeping track of final awards.*
12. A list of cats competing,* separated by class into:
    Longhair Kitten Class
    Shorthair Kitten Class
    Longhair Championship Class
    Shorthair Championship Class

Longhair Alter/Premier Class
Shorthair Alter/Premier Class
Household Pets

This list is divided alphabetically by breed, and provides space for you to keep track of what the judge does with each cat and each group of cats (HHPs are sometimes divided into longhair and shorthair classes, unless the sponsoring federation judges all HHPs as All-Breeds).

13. An absentee and change list.*
14. A list of exhibitors with their addresses.
15. A judging schedule for Saturday and Sunday.* This lists the number of each ring, which judge will be judging in that ring, whether the ring is a Specialty or an All-Breed ring, and a list of the order in which the cats will be judged (sometimes including an approximate time the judging will take place).

Always check the catalog for your cat's entry immediately. The information in the catalog must be corrected right away if it is wrong, because a copy of this catalog is used by the master clerk to keep track of how each cat scored at the show. At the end of the show, the catalog, completely marked, is sent to the federation's regional and national scorekeepers. It is then compared with the judges' books and the total score for your cat is kept by the federation. If there is a correction needed in the catalog information, talk to the master clerk. Even a small error can be important. For example, if your cat's registration number is correct, but the name is wrong, the federation keeping track of the results may not be able to post your cat's wins and points quickly (or ever). Remember, they are keeping track of the progress of thousands of cats each year.

The catalog is a permanent record of the shows in which your cat was judged. When you get a show flyer in the future, you can go back to your catalogs and see how a particular judge scored your cat. This can help you decide which shows to enter.

THE ABSENTEE AND CHANGE LIST

In the show catalog, you will find a list for marking the absentees and changes. In some federations, a specialty field of fewer than twenty-five cats will only permit the top five cats to Final. Any absences in your specialty are, therefore, very important to you.

Cats are removed for many different reasons. Some active exhibitors will "double enter" shows. This means that they will enter two shows

The spectators' area from the judge's side of the table. Note the spray bottles of disinfectant to be used after each cat is judged.

A steward cleans and disinfects each cage before a new cat is placed in it.

GRC Thesaurus Con Brio of Citylights, a Male Red Point Himalayan, is combed by owner H. Stephen Joostema before judging.

This beautiful Chinchilla Persian kitten, Suttonian Etiahna, gets a final grooming before being judged.

that are being held on the same weekend. After the show has closed, they will call the Entry Clerk to get the "Championship count." This count tells them how many cats are entered in the Championship class. They may then choose to go to the show with the higher Championship count. This enables them to get more points for the cats they defeat. This is very important when you are campaigning a cat for regional or national recognition.

An exhibitor may pull a cat for other reasons. If you are showing a longhair cat, such as a Persian, your cat may "blow its coat." If you are showing a kitten, or a young cat who is still growing, you may find that your cat is going through a growing phase and has temporarily grown away from the Standard of Perfection by which the breed is judged. If you feel the show would be a wasted effort, you may choose to pull your cat (be absent) rather than show a cat not looking its best.

In addition to absences, some cats may have changed status between shows. While a cat may have entered the show as an "Open," it may have achieved a Championship at another show. The status is now changed from Open to Champion and the cat will compete that way.

THE GROOMING CALL

Most head ring clerks will announce a "grooming call" for the cats that are to be called up to the ring next to be judged. This gives you time to do a little last-minute grooming of your cat before taking it to the ring to be judged without delaying all the other exhibitors by coming to the ring late.

Before you take your cat to the judging ring, check to make sure the cat didn't mess itself up. Always check:

- The ears (making certain they are still clean and look properly trimmed).
- The eyes (making certain they are clean and not tearing).
- The nose (for cleanliness).
- The face in general (for cleanliness and to make certain there are no tear stains).
- The bottom (to make certain the cat is clean).
- The coat (to make certain it is free of tangles, is shiny, clean and looks perfectly groomed).

This is the last chance you have to handle your cat before it is judged, so make any last-minute repairs to your grooming that are needed. Unfortunately, sometimes a grooming call will not be given at all, or not

When your cat's number is called, take it to the judging ring and place it in the cage with the appropriate number on the top. Before you put the cat in, feel the bottom of the cage to make sure it has been adequately dried after being cleaned and disinfected.

These cats have all been caged in the judging ring, after being called for Finals.

TICA All-Breed judge Gloria Stephens cleans and disinfects her hands and the judging table before judging the next cat.

Sassy stands still while being handled by the judge.

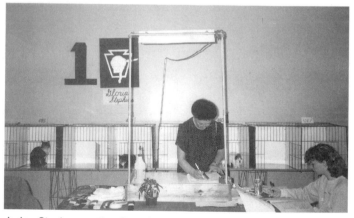

Judge Stephens writes Sassy's score in the judge's book after she is judged. Ring clerk Susan Angermeyer checks the judge's scoring.

for the judgings of shorthair cats in the various classes. If that happens when you are exhibiting a shorthair cat, rely upon the judging schedule to allow yourself enough time to groom your cat before the ring.

CARRYING YOUR CAT TO THE JUDGING RING

Your cat will let you know how it wants to be carried to the ring. Some cats prefer being carried close to the owner, while others like showing off by being carried high above the owner's head. Some cats like having their eyes covered by the owner's hand, so they don't have to see the crowd, while others seem to thrive on seeing so many people. No matter how you carry your cat, make sure to hold the cat *securely*. While you may see exhibitors letting their cat ride on their shoulder to and from the judging rings, this is not a good idea. If something spooks the cat, it can easily jump down and run to find a place to hide. For this and other reasons, sometimes a show committee will suggest that all cats be brought to the rings in a carrier. If this is the case, by all means, bring your cat to the ring in a travel cage.

Unless the show committee requests that cats be brought to the judging rings in carriers, try to carry your cat by hand. In fact, there are some judges who will not handle a cat they see being brought up in a carrier. They assume that the exhibitor can't handle the cat and may disqualify the cat without ever touching it.

CAGING YOUR CAT IN THE JUDGING RING

When you have reached the judging ring, you will find numbers on top of the judging cages. The cards the numbers are on are either pink or blue— pink designating a female (or spayed) cat and blue designating a male (or neutered) cat. If your cat is a female and the number on the cage is on a blue card, or vice versa, tell the ring clerk before you cage your cat. The clerk may tell you to just reverse the card or may move you to another cage.

In the Championship class, male and female cats are placed in alternate cages. If the field is mostly male cats, they will be separated by an empty cage. This may or may not hold true in the Kitten, Alter/Premier and HHP classes. That depends on the individual judge and his or her experience with kittens and neutered cats. If the judge feels the kittens may have matured early, males will be separated. If, in the judge's

Two Abyssinian cats look around after the cage curtains have been removed from their cage at the end of the show.

Exhibitors at the Garden State Cat Club (NJ) show, traditionally one of the largest CFA shows in the country.

experience, castrated males never lose the feeling of being a whole male, then these cats will be separated also.

Sometimes you will find two cats that are benched in adjoining judging cages that seem to develop an immediate and intense dislike of each other. They may hiss or try to get around the cage to get at each other. If this is the case, ask the ring clerk to separate the cats before he or she puts up cage cards. If the ring clerk can, he or she will try to accommodate you as this is not an uncommon situation.

At most shows, you get to the judging cages by going behind the judge and opening the cage from the front. If you have to cage your cat this way, be sure to stay out of the judge's way. Sometimes you will find cages that open both in the front (on the judge's side of the ring) and in the back. If these cages are being used, cage your cat from the back of the ring. Some clubs set up the judging rings with special aisles for the exhibitors to use. These shows have usually been found to be very crowded, with many spectators, and the show committee has determined that this is the best way for the exhibitors to cage their cats for judging. If you find a show like this, follow the instructions of the show committee and bench your cat in the judging ring the way you are directed.

EXHIBITORS' RESPONSIBILITIES DURING JUDGING

You should always try to *stay at*, but *not in*, the ring when your cat is being judged. If this is not possible, have someone you trust, who knows the cat stay there for you.

Unless the judge asks for the owner, never talk to the judge. Most federations have a rule that prohibits exhibitors from talking to a judge unless the judge initiates the conversation. Sometimes the judge will want to ask the owner a question. At other times, a cat may become very hard to handle. In this instance, the judge may request that the owner take the cat from the judging cage and put it on the judging table. If the cat is still not calm, the judge may instruct the owner to talk to the cat or show a toy to calm the cat down so it can be judged. It must be possible to handle a cat if it is to be judged.

9

The Judging Process

THE JUDGING OF cats, or anything else, is a mixture of objectivity and subjectivity. In judging pedigreed cats, there is a Standard of Perfection to guide the judges' evaluations. However, that Standard is subject to each judge's interpretation of the written words. Judging Household Pet cats further allows freedom of judgment, as many intangibles come into play. For these reasons cat shows are best enjoyed when exhibitors realize that judges, like the rest of us, are all too human.

WHAT A JUDGE LOOKS FOR IN JUDGING
A PUREBRED CAT

A judge must rate a purebred cat against the Standard of Perfection for the breed. The Standard starts with the members of the breed council or breed committee. This is a group made up of federation members, who are breeders of a particular breed (each federation has rules for determining who is eligible to serve on a breed council). After the breed council has designed the Standard, it is sent out to the breed section members for voting. The members of the breed section are members of the federation who are interested in that particular breed but who are not members of the breed council. If the Standard is accepted by the majority of those eligible to vote on it, it is accepted and used as the judging Standard for that federation.

The Standard describes, in detail, what a particular breed must look

A portrait of SGC Edmars Allison. *David Eckard*

TICA All-Breed judge Karen
McInchak lets Sassy check
out the judging table.

Judge McInchak
holds Sassy up so
the crowd can see her
markings.

TICA All-Breed judge Don Shaw has a word with Gaiety after making her his Best HHP.

Judge Shaw shows Gaiety to the spectators.

like. All aspects of the cat are covered, both general features and those unique to the breed. The Standard also designates which colors and color patterns are considered acceptable in that breed, and which colors and color patterns are *not* acceptable for that breed.

Because cats change, so do breed Standards, both as they are written and as they are interpreted. Twenty years ago, you would not have seen many Persian cats with flat faces. Now, that is part of the Standard of the breed. Also, many more color variations are acceptable in some breeds now than in the past.

What the cat show judge does is apply that breed Standard to each cat judged. The judge mentally rates the cat against the Standard ("twenty out of twenty-five possible points for the head, thirty points for the body, ten points for the coat, thirty out of thirty-five points for color, for a total of ninety points out of a possible one hundred for this Abyssinian"), then against any other cats of the same color and division, and then against all other cats of the same breed. This determines the cat considered best in each class, each color, each division and each breed. In determining the top five or ten cats from among the longhairs, the shorthairs or all cats, the judge essentially judges all the cats that were the best two or three in their breed against each other.

WHAT A JUDGE LOOKS FOR IN JUDGING AN HHP

An HHP is something special in the cat world. Originally, the term probably referred to any cat of unknown origin—that is, your basic alley or shelter cat. But now, it has come to include more. An HHP is a cat judged with other HHPs. It may be the offspring of two registered, purebred cats, with an impressive pedigree of its own. But, *and this is important*, it does not meet the breed Standard in some respect. This does not mean the cat is not beautiful and loved. What it means is that, if judged against others of the same breed, this cat would not be considered good enough to Champion.

That is why you may see what are called "apparent purebreds" in the Household Pet ring. They may, in fact, *be* purebreds, but their owners have decided to show them as HHPs. That is not a black mark against them. It just means that they are being shown in one group, and not in another.

All federations allow cat shows to have HHP rings. And the fact that the fastest-growing segment of the average cat show is the HHP group is additional testimony to their importance at cat shows.

Some federations, and some judges, set great store on the personality

Audrey Kriston, ACFA All-Breed judge, judges an Exotic Shorthair cat.

ACFA All-Breed judge Ken Miller judges an American Curl cat in the NBC ring. (NBC stands for "New Breed or Color." This ring may also be called AOV, standing for "Any Other Variety.") The NBC ring is the only ring where the exhibitor can explain the breed Standards to the judge. This ring enables the judge to learn what the breeders are doing with a new breed.

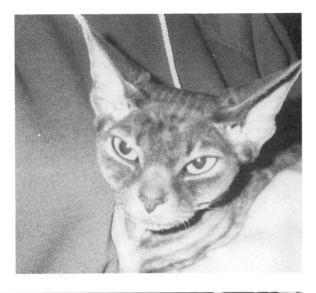

Quadruple Champion Moorelves Sabrina Fair, a Blue McTabby Devon Rex, shows off her butterfly ears while resting in the arms of owner Hilary Ingalls.

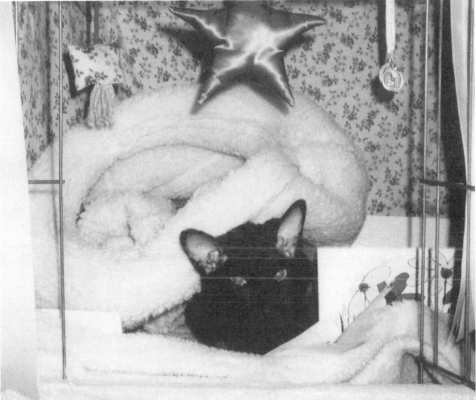

Champion Typha Bump in the Nite of Alchemy, an Ebony Oriental Shorthair Alter owned by Sue Hansen, relaxes under his bed during the show.

A Turkish Angora, GRC Darmax's Sweet Silver Belle, at her benching cage.

This Silver Somali, owned by Abbie Carbine, is the first full pedigreed female of that breed and color in the United States. Philomenea was bred in West Germany.

of the cat being shown in the HHP ring. This can be true whether or not the personality of the cat is officially part of the breed Standards. This is why you will want your HHP to be completely socialized and able to be easily handled in the ring.

A judge has more leeway in judging Household Pets than in judging purebred cats, even though some federations include a written Standard of Perfection for an HHP. After determining that the HHP is impeccably clean and healthy, the judge can be attracted by anything he or she particularly enjoys seeing in a cat. Some judges are known for being particularly attracted to tabbies or to calico cats. Sometimes, when the judge is awarding Final rosettes to HHPs, he or she will tell you why a cat was awarded Best HHP. This is always interesting to hear. Most judges enjoy judging the HHP ring because it permits them to have fun with the cats and select their top ten because of something that strikes their fancy.

HOW A JUDGE INTERPRETS THE STANDARDS

Judges go through extensive training before they are allowed to judge a cat show on their own. And, in most federations, they must take a review test every year. The best judges also take advantage of the frequent breed seminars sponsored by the various federations or breed Fancies to learn more about all of the breeds they see, and particularly about breeds they do not see very often (sometimes called "minority breeds").

One of the things judges must learn is to apply the Standards of Perfection. The Standards, as they are written, may appear somewhat vague. When in the ring, the judge is really interpreting the Standard in the way he or she was taught. For example, the ACFA Standard of Perfection for the Persian cat states that the back (of the body) should be "short and level with a well-rounded mid-section," and that the tail "should be short but in proportion to the body length." The judge is taught to interpret this part of the Standard in the following manner: The length of the body, measured from the top of the shoulders (withers) to the beginning of the tail, should equal the height of the cat from withers to ground. The length of the tail should also equal the length of the body as described above.

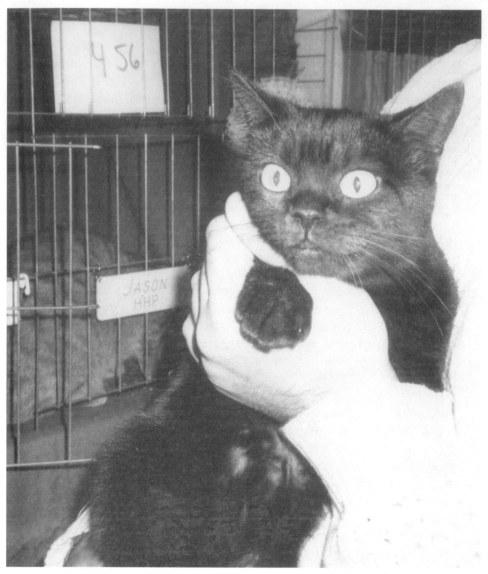

Lady Artemus, a Black Smoke HHP, is owned and loved by N. Alan Gehman.

A Persian kitten, offered for sale at a show by Helen Case, plays with a toy.

Dr. James Williams plays with his blue and white HHP, SGM Little Orphan Andy.

WHEN A JUDGE LOOKS UP STANDARDS

Sometimes judges will be faced with judging a breed of cat they have never seen before, or haven't seen in quite a while. In this case, you may see the judge take out the book of Standards and review it. It is a good idea for the judge to occasionally review the Standard of Perfection for a breed instead of relying upon memory. As more and more breeds of cats are accepted for judging in the Championship class, and as the Standards for older breeds are changed, you can't really expect a judge to know everything about every Standard for every breed.

DISQUALIFICATIONS

Sometimes you will see a cat disqualified from being judged in the class in which it is entered. Sometimes this is for a technical reason— for example, the color of the cat may not be accepted by that particular federation for judging in the Championship class. Even if the reason is not a technical one, disqualifications do occur.

More and more, judges are being encouraged to disqualify cats that do not substantially meet the breed Standard. This is because one of the purposes of cat federations is to encourage the breeding of quality pure-bred cats. The judges feel a cat that does not meet the breed standard should not be shown. If shown, the cat may achieve a title, particularly in those federations where only winner's ribbons earn the cat the title of "Champion." If the cat earns a title, it may eventually be bred. If bred, it may produce only pet-quality kittens, or even pass on a genetic defect. This, of course, is unfair to the cat, the kittens, any future owners of the kittens and the breed itself. It also contributes to the cat overpopulation problem.

Sometimes a judge will suggest that the cat be transferred to another class—for example, from the Alter/Premier class to the HHP class. This way the cat can still be judged, but in the class where it really belongs. What is considered a breed defect in a Championship cat or an Alter/Premier can be very appealing in an HHP. Transferring the cat to the HHP class also assures that the cat will be neutered, because cats competing in this class must be neutered to be shown.

THE JUDGING PROCEDURE

By the time judges take a cat out of the cage and get it to the judging table, they have already done a lot of judging. They have already felt

Silkie Su's Che-Ears To You is a Longhair Scottish Fold. This breed is accepted for Championship competition in TICA, but in CFF it is considered an "AOV." "AOV" is a Non-Championship class of purebred cats.

the weight of the cat, some of the bone and the coat texture. Now the cat is examined closely, on the judging table, for the characteristics of its breed. For example, the judge now examines the head for shape and profile, the shape of the eye and the eyeball, the set of the ears (flaring or close to the head and rounded), the mouth and muzzle, the body and tail length and the overall appearance of the cat, including stance. A judge may then hold the cat up to the light for a final look at coat and eye color.

Sometimes you will see a judge tempt the cat with a cat toy while the animal is on the judging table. This is usually done so that the judge can observe the muscles and body structure of the cat in action. For some judges, it is also an extra moment of play.

Once the cat is back in the judging cage, particularly if there are many cats of the same breed being judged, the judge will stand back to look at all the cats next to each other. When the review of the cats is complete, either one at a time or as a group, the judge marks their scores in the judge's book, awards the "flats," releases the cats from the ring, and continues judging.

Finals

After the judge has judged all the cats, he or she then determines the top five or top ten cats (depending upon whether it is a Specialty or an All-Breed ring, and on the federation rules). These are the top cats in the field, in that judge's opinion. There will be an announcement that Finals are being held in that ring. Some federations announce the numbers of the cats in the Finals. In other federations, the numbers are posted on the judging ring cages, and exhibitors are expected to check to see if their cat's number is there. If your cat's number is posted or announced, take your cat to the judging ring and place it in the appropriate cage. Don't hold up the Finals presentation with elaborate grooming; a quick grooming will have to do.

Once all the cats are benched for Finals, the judge will announce the top cats, starting from the bottom of the Finalists and moving up to the Best Cat for that ring. Sometimes the judge will ask the exhibitors to present their cats. If this is requested, take your cat out of the cage when your number is called and hold the cat for the audience to see. If the judge is talking about the Standards, try to hold the cat so the audience can see what the judge is talking about. For example, when presenting a Japanese Bobtail, hold the cat so the audience can admire the characteristic pom-pom tail. Once the Final award has been presented, replace your cat in the judging cage and return to your seat.

Ron Summers, ACFA All-Breed judge, signs the back of the rosettes before the presentation of Finals. Many judges do this for the exhibitors.

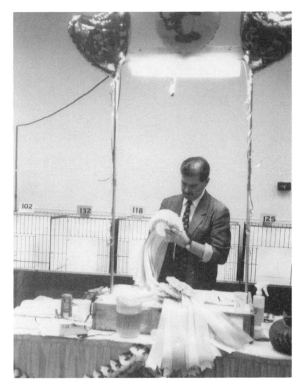

A Finals rosette is designed by the club sponsoring the show.

ACFA All-Breed judge Robert Zenda awards a Finals rosette to Kiri.

A wall of many-colored rosettes can be enjoyed each time you pass by it.

After all the Final awards have been presented, the cats will be released. It is appropriate at this time to thank the judge. If you like, you may ask the judge to sign the rosette.

Don't get discouraged if you do not make a Final on your first ring. Each judge interprets the Standards a little differently, or there may be something special he or she is looking for in a certain breed. The next judge may very well place your cat in the Finals. Also, the field of cats being judged changes from show to show. That one judge failed to give your cat a Final in one show doesn't mean that judge will never Final your cat. Conversely, that a judge gave you a Final in one show doesn't mean you should count on getting a Final every time. The one time the Finals results don't change very much is when a judge is judging a Specialty ring one day of the show, and judging an All-Breed ring the other day. This is known as "back-to-back judging." Unless the field changes drastically, the Finals on the second day will (and should) be very consistent with those of the first day's judging.

DO POLITICS AFFECT CAT JUDGING?

Showing cats involves dealing with many people. And, believe it or not, judges are people too. No one can like everybody, and not everybody in the cat world will become your friend. Showing cats is very competitive and, unfortunately, not everyone is a good competitor. Some people get very upset when their cat doesn't do as well as they expected, so they look for someone to blame. The easiest person to blame is the judge.

Some exhibitors blame *everything* on politics. They may be ignoring the fact that their cat is not as good as the other cats being shown, or even that the cat doesn't meet the breed Standard. It is from those people that you will often hear the lament that the judge "dumped" their cat. What they mean is that in their opinion their cat had a "right" to Final, but did not.

Politics in the world of cat exhibiting does not benefit anyone.

You may hear it said that one federation is superior to another because the breeders and exhibitors are more professional, or the quality of the cats is better. Every federation has its "good" judges and its "bad" judges. To some people, whether judges are good or bad usually depends on whether or not they have put their cat in the Finals.

The people who show cats in all federations tend to be friendly and helpful. You must realize that as a newcomer to showing cats, or as a newcomer to a particular federation, you are running into people who may have known each other and exhibited together for many years. It may take a couple of shows for you to make friends, but you will make friends with more and more people the longer you show cats. There is a lot of time between judging rings during a cat show. Exhibitors tend to talk to each other, wander around the showhall, buy supplies and look at each other's cats. In this way, you get to know people. At first you will only know people by breed ("Oh, yes, you're the Turkish Angora"), but eventually, you will know them by name. At that point, the cat show can turn into a happy, social occasion as well as a competition.

10

Awards—How They Are Earned and What They Mean

TECHNICALLY, a "cat" is an adult pedigreed cat being judged as such. An adult is any cat at least eight months old *at the time the show is held*, not when you enter it. That is not the same as an "Alter" or "Premier," which is a cat over the age of eight months that has been "spayed" (if female) or "neutered" (if male). Sometimes they are called "Spays" or "Neuters" at the show. A "kitten" is a pedigreed cat under the age of eight months, but at least four months old.

"Household Pet" or "HHP" usually means any other cat, over the age of eight months, that has been fixed. In some federations, that also includes HHP kittens—that is, kittens over the age of four months (which do not necessarily have to have been fixed yet), but under eight months old. In other federations, HHP kittens are judged against each other. While originally HHPs were expected to be cats of unknown origin, now all federations allow you to show as an HHP any cat that is pedigreed, but that is less than perfect according to the federation's standards.

SCORING

Scoring cat shows requires you to pay close attention. Each federation and each breed group has its own set of rules on scoring (see

ALL BREED

RING NO. _____ JUDGE _____

| | CHAMPION | | | HOUSEHOLD PET | |
	CATS	ALTERS	KITTENS	CATS	KITTENS
BEST CAT					
2nd BEST					
3rd BEST					
4th BEST					
5th BEST					
6th BEST					
7th BEST					
8th BEST					
9th BEST					
10th BEST					

		CATS	ALTERS
LONGHAIR	BEST		
	2ND		
SHORTHAIR	BEST		
	2ND		
MASTER GRAND	BEST		
	2ND		
GRAND CHAMPION	BEST		
	2ND		
CHAMPION	BEST		
	2ND		
LH CHAMP	BEST		
	2ND		
SH CHAMP	BEST		
	2ND		
NOVICE	BEST		
	2ND		

		CATS	ALTERS
AOV	BEST		
	2ND		
EXPERIMENTAL	BEST		
	2ND		

| | CHAMPION | | ALTER | |
	BEST	2ND	BEST	2ND
BALINESE				
BIRMAN				
HIMALAYAN				
KASHMIR				
MAINE COON				
NOR. FOREST				
PERSIAN				
RAGDOLL				
SOMALI				
TURKISH ANGORA				
ABYSSINIAN				
AMERICAN SH				
BOMBAY				
BRITISH SH				
BURMESE				
CHARTREUX				
CORNISH REX				
DEVON REX				
EGYPTIAN MAU				
EXOTIC SH				
HAVANA BROWN				
JAPANESE BOBTAIL				
KORAT				
MANX				
ORIENTAL SH				
RUSSIAN BLUE				
SCOTTISH FOLD				
SIAMESE				
SINGAPURA				
SNOWSHOE				
TONKINESE				

CFF Finals pages.

LONGHAIR

RING NO. _____ JUDGE _____

| | CHAMPION | | | HOUSEHOLD PET | |
	CATS	ALTERS	KITTENS	CATS	KITTENS
BEST CAT					
2nd BEST					
3rd BEST					
4th BEST					
5th BEST					
6th BEST					
7th BEST					
8th BEST					
9th BEST					
10th BEST					

| | CHAMPION | | ALTER | |
	BEST	2ND	BEST	2ND
BALINESE				
BIRMAN				
HIMALAYAN				
KASHMIR				
MAINE COON				
NORWEIGN FOREST				
PERSIAN				
RAGDOLL				
SOMALI				
TURKISH ANGORA				

		CATS	ALTERS
MASTER GRAND	BEST		
	2ND		
GRAND CHAMPION	BEST		
	2ND		
CHAMPION	BEST		
	2ND		
NOVICE	BEST		
	2ND		

		CATS	ALTERS
AOV	BEST		
	2ND		
EXPERIMENTAL	BEST		
	2ND		

SHORTHAIR

RING NO. _____ JUDGE _____

| | CHAMPION | | | HOUSEHOLD PET | |
	CATS	ALTERS	KITTENS	CATS	KITTENS
BEST CAT					
2nd BEST					
3rd BEST					
4th BEST					
5th BEST					
6th BEST					
7th BEST					
8th BEST					
9th BEST					
10th BEST					

| | CHAMPION | | ALTER | |
	BEST	2ND	BEST	2ND
ABYSSINIAN				
AMERICAN SH				
BOMBAY				
BRITISH SH				
BURMESE				
CHARTREUX				
CORNISH REX				
DEVON REX				
EGYPTIAN MAU				
EXOTIC SH				
HAVANA BROWN				
JAPANESE BOBTAIL				
KORAT				
MANX				
ORIENTAL SH				
RUSSIAN BLUE				
SCOTTISH FOLD				
SIAMESE				
SINGAPURA				
SNOWSHOE				
TONKINESE				

		CATS	ALTERS
MASTER GRAND	BEST		
	2ND		
GRAND CHAMPION	BEST		
	2ND		
CHAMPION	BEST		
	2ND		
NOVICE	BEST		
	2ND		

		CATS	ALTERS
AOV	BEST		
	2ND		
EXPERIMENTAL	BEST		
	2ND		

appendices). While they differ somewhat, they are all variations of one or more of the following:

- Your cat earns points for meeting a written Standard.
- Your cat receives points for defeating other cats, starting from those of the same color, pattern and breed all the way up to all breeds and all colors.
- Your cat may earn points based on the number of cats defeated. In some federations, that means the number of cats in competition that the judge actually sees to judge ("handled" or "judged"); in others, it means all cats that are actually in the show hall ("benched"), whether or not the judge actually saw them.

In general, a cat must earn its points and awards in the same class, division or color class.

If your cat earned a title as an "entire" cat, and afterward you have it altered, in some federations you can transfer the titles so that you have them when the cat is later shown as an Alter.

Points can be accumulated only by cats that are already registered with the sponsoring federation. However, in some cases, you can take a cat to *one* show without registering it and then claim the points after the show by immediately registering the cat with the federation sponsoring the show.

Additionally, there are other regulations governing the earning of points which may vary with the federation:

- Points are awarded only for defeating certain, but not all, cats.
- Points are counted only for a maximum number of competitions.
- You may have to accumulate your points or wins under a minimum number of different judges.
- Points awarded in a category are not counted for all purposes.
- As you go for higher and higher titles, it is progressively more difficult to accumulate points.
- Points for awards by breed associations may sometimes be acceptable only when awarded by certain federations.
- You may sometimes be able to transfer wins from one association to another, although this is possible less and less often.

If you do need to accumulate points or wins under a minimum number of different judges, a curious question may arise: When is the same judge a different judge? If you come to a cat show and one of the judges listed in the catalog is not able to judge, the show committee will try to replace the judge so the complete show can continue. If your cat earns points or flats from the replacement judge, most federations will let you consider that judge as "a different judge." Let us give you an example. Let's say that you have already received three winner's ribbons in ACFA, from judges Smith, Brown and Green. That means you need one more from a different judge for a championship. Now Judge Williams becomes ill at the show and is replaced by Judge Brown. Judge Brown then gives your cat another winner's ribbon. Do you have your four winner's ribbons from four different judges? Yes. The emergency replacement may be a kind of wild card for you.

If this happens and the judge's action is important to you, make sure you find out from someone at the show if this is the case. When it can happen depends on the federation, its rules for titles and the circumstances under which the replacement was made.

MARKING YOUR CATALOG

When you look at your catalog, you will find that for every cat in the show, there is a wealth of information, some of it cryptic. While there is some variation between federations, the typical entry in the show catalog contains the following:

- The cat's registered name.
- The cat's registration number, *in the federation sponsoring the show*.
- The breeders of the cat.
- The owners of the cat.
- The agent showing the cat, if any.
- The cat's sire and dam.
- The cat's birth date.
- The cat's age at the time of the show.
- Some indication of the region in which the cat's owners live.
- The cat's color and pattern.
- The breed, division, class and so forth to which the cat has been assigned, and with which it will be judged.
- The cat's current status, such as Open, Novice, Champion or Companion.
- The number assigned to that cat for this show.

When you step back at the ring from putting your cat in its cage, you will see many exhibitors marking their catalogs, even if their own cats are not yet being judged. What they are doing is keeping track of other cats in the show. Also, while you may not be able to see it, the ring clerk is also marking up a catalog, keeping track of everything that

ORIENTAL SHORTHAIR KITTEN

OSHT27MK - RED MC TABBY MALE KITTEN

```
           21   SUE-MC OLDE SPICE                21
--- --- --- --- --- KIT              2/2/89      KIT --- --- --- --- ---
                GC SUE-MC MY SIN
                SUE-MC JOY
                SUE MC KENNEY
                SUE MC KENNEY  AG: J.VIEL
```


SCOTTISH FOLD KITTENS

SFH33FK - TORTIE HARLEQUIN FEMALE KITTEN

```
           22   SILVER NUGGETTES MC SPARKLE      22
--- --- --- --- --- KIT   SFH33F2-92999   3/27/89   KIT --- --- --- --- ---
                CH MC TARRBY OF SILVER NUGGETTES
                SILVER NUGGETTES MC FIESTA
                NANCIE S BELSER
                NANCIE S BELSER
```


SF50EMK - BROWN TABBY/WHITE MALE KITTEN

```
           23   ALBANNACH'S CHECKERS             23
--- --- --- --- --- KIT              5/15/89      KIT --- --- --- --- ---
                ROB ROY OF ALBANNACH (SF82M1-86567)
                ALBANNACH'S EALASAID (SF100F2-93151)
                BEVERLEY HARDACRE
                BEVERLEY HARDACRE
```


SF82FK - BLACK SMOKE/WHITE FEMALE KITTEN

```
           24   SILKIE SU'S DAISY MAE            24
--- --- --- --- --- KIT   SF82F2-93411   2/19/89   KIT --- --- --- --- ---
                CH SILVER NUGGETTES MC FARLEY
                BRYRIC SALLY OF SILKIE SU
                SUSAN STEPHENS
                SUE ROSS
```

A page from a CFF show catalog.

A flat ribbon indicates how your cat did in preliminary judging.

Soon, all of these will have been given to some lucky cats.

the judge does with each cat. And, out of your sight entirely, the master clerk is keeping track of what is happening in every ring. In fact, the national office of the federation sponsoring the show will be getting a copy of the catalog, marked to show what happened at the show, often within two days after the show is over.

How is the catalog usually used? To understand this, you have to know about the layout of the catalog. First, next to each entry in the catalog, you will see a series of short lines. At the top of each page, above the column of lines, are initials. What this does is provide a place next to the name of each cat, and under initials representing each judge, for you to keep track of what happens to your cat.

Then you will notice that there are separate lines, clustered at the end of groups of cats. These lines are there to allow you to keep track of how various cats do against each other.

Now, how should you use the catalog to keep track of what your cat does? The answer is that you should feel free to mark up your catalog in any way you want, just so that you understand it and can make sense of it later. You see, you may have to rely on that catalog to come up with the information needed to file a confirmation to get your cat a title.

FLATS AND RIBBONS

In all federations' shows, judges mark results using what are known as "flats" to indicate awards. These take their name from their origin as flat ribbons or printed paper strips, as distinguished from rosettes or trophies, which the cat's owner took back with the cat. In each federation, specific colors have been assigned to most of these awards.

Increasingly, clubs are substituting "super flats" for ribbon flats. Super flats are colored hard plastic awards placed at the cage, indicating the judge's decision. They are used over and over by the judges, and are not to be taken back to your cage. If you want to take a flat back, they will usually be available from the clerk at the ring or at the announcer's or master clerk's table.

The flats formerly always carried a written statement on them, indicating what they were for—that is, "Merit," "Second-Best of Breed" and so forth. Now some flats and super flats may only carry an abbreviation—for example, "1C," which indicates the award is for the First of Color. In some shows, the super flats do not even carry that kind of cryptic notation.

To help you sort out what the colors mean, we have provided tables

Trophies and special rosettes are presented to the overall winners in the show. This award is known as the "Best of the Best."

Pataron Morning Star of Shennaught is on her way to becoming Best of the Best Kitten in the Show. This Tortie Persian is owned by Pat and Jim Gresham.

in the appendices listing the most important flats for each of the four federations.

BEST OF THE BEST AWARDS

The Best of the Best Cat, Kitten, Alter/Premier and Household Pet are given to the cat who scored highest in that particular category in all the rings at that show. This is determined by adding the scores of all the cats who competed in that particular class.

At most shows, the Best of the Best Awards are presented at the end of the show. Even if you will not be receiving a Best of the Best, you should try to stay to see the presentation, although that is not required. This is a very exciting presentation as it is an award highly prized by all exhibitors. The rosettes presented for the Best of the Best are quite beautiful.

BEST IN SHOW AWARD

The Best in Show Award is usually given only at major shows, such as those sponsored by INCATS (affiliated with TICA). To determine the Best in Show, the show officials must first determine which cat is the highest-scoring cat in each particular breed. This finding is based upon the cumulative scores of all the cats that competed in each breed.

The cats that scored highest in their breed are then judged against each other by judges who have not judged during the show at all. This is akin to an All-Breed judging ring, which has only one representative of each breed present and competing. Also, the cats may be judged by more than one judge in order to arrive at a consensus. When all the cats have been judged, a Final is held and the Best in Show is named.

Needless to say, this is a very special ring and a very special occasion. The awards presented to those cats named as the best of their breed are special and the award for the Best in Show is spectacular. This is as much fun to watch as a spectator as it is if you are lucky enough to be a participant.

MORRIS ANIMAL FOUNDATION BEST KITTEN AWARD

This award, given to purebred kittens by the Morris Animal Foundation, is designed to remind owners and breeders that the Morris Animal

The master clerk takes the total points accumulated by the cats judged in every ring and totals them to get the overall winners of the show.

TICA gives special rosettes to the cats that place in the top twenty at the regional level. Note the name of the cat imprinted on the streamer.

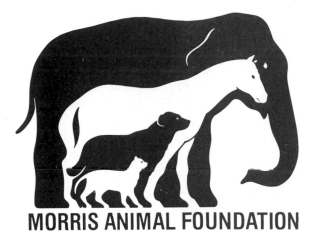

The Morris Animal Foundation logo.
© 1989.

The Morris Animal Foundation
sponsors an award for purebred kittens.   © 1989

Foundation is working to prevent the diseases and health problems that affect cats right from the beginning—when they're kittens—and all through life.

It is intended for the Best Kitten in the senior judge's All-Breed ring or the kitten with the highest score in all rings for Best of the Best Kitten. The winner is given a response form to fill out and return. Information from this form is compiled and at the end of the year the kitten that won the most shows is named Kitten of the Year. The first Kitten of the Year presentation was made at the Foundation's 1988 annual meeting in Denver, Colorado. The winner was Pataron's Alysheba, a black Persian, owned by Ms. Pat Milligan of Florida.

THE 9-LIVES MORRIS AWARD

First awarded in 1973, the Morris Award (not to be confused with the Morris Animal Foundation) is the most coveted award of Household Pet exhibitors. The award is presented by the 9-Lives Cat Food Company to the winner of the Best Household Pet competition at approximately 450 cat shows nationwide each year. The trophy is a bronze likeness of the Most Finicky One, Morris, the 9-Lives Cat. It's only fitting that the trophy is made by the same company that makes the "Oscar" for humans.

The Morris Award was created by 9-Lives Cat Food Company in honor of its finicky spokescat, Morris, to recognize beauty and excellence in nonpedigreed cats. Morris himself was a humble stray before 9-Lives rescued him and turned him into a star. The Morris Award gives non-pedigreed cats everywhere a chance to shine.

More than five thousand Morris Awards have been presented since its 1973 premiere at a Chicago cat show. Morris himself has awarded the trophy at many shows, including shows in Los Angeles, New York City and Chicago.

THE 9-LIVES BEST HOUSEHOLD KITTEN AWARD

This award was created by 9-Lives to recognize the beauty of Household Pet kittens. The award gives kitten owners something to work for until their cats can be eligible for the Morris Award at age eight months.

The 9-Lives Best Household Kitten Award is a red and white rosette bearing a photograph of Morris the Cat.

Editor's Note: As we go to press, the 9-Lives Company announces that, after sixteen years, the 9-Lives Morris Awards will end May 1, 1990.

The 9-Lives Company's spokescat, Morris, and the trophy that bears his name.

HAPPY HOUSEHOLD PET CAT CLUB ROSETTES

The Happy Household Pet Cat Club (HHPCC) is a national cat club devoted to HHPs. The club registers HHPs, publishes a newsletter, gives annual national awards and produces a yearbook. HHPCC recognizes the beauty of HHPs by giving rosettes in the HHP ring at sanctioned cat shows when it has the cooperation of the sponsoring club.

These beautiful purple and white rosettes carry the logo of the Happy Household Pet Cat Club. They are given to the Best Cat in the senior All-Breed judge's ring. Sometimes they are given in more than one ring.

BREED ASSOCIATION AWARDS

Sometimes you will see a card on the cage of the cats who have scored Best (or Best and Second-Best) in a particular breed in the Champion, Alter and Kitten rings. These are breed association or breed group awards.

Each recognized breed has one or more breed associations to which owners, exhibitors and breeders of that particular breed can belong. This is like a specialized cat club and is devoted to that breed only, or even to one type of cat within a particular breed. Typically, they try to honor cats of their breed at federation-sanctioned shows through awards at each show and national and regional recognition.

At some shows, you will see the judge put a special card or ribbon on the cages of some cats, kittens or Alters, such as the Best Maine Coon Kitten or the Second-Best Himalayan Cat. These are provided by the breed groups to be given at a show by some or all judges. They carry no special points or benefits for the winner in the federation sponsoring the show, but may within the breed group.

PRIVATELY GIVEN AWARDS

Some cat federations permit individuals to donate special awards to a club's shows. These awards are usually in memory of a particular cat, and they are designated that way. For example, we give the following special awards annually: the Pansy Award to the Best Tabby HHP, the Kali Award to the Best Calico HHP, the Hashi Award to the Best Shaded HHP and the Prissi Award to the Best Pointed HHP.

Special awards are not limited to the Household Pet ring. We have seen awards given to the highest-scoring Alter, the highest-scoring Himalayan, the highest-scoring cat in the Championship Ring and the oldest cat in the show.

These awards are extremely special to the donor. They give the donor an opportunity to share that very special cat with another person. It is remembered by the donor, by everyone at the show, whether they knew the cat or not, and by the recipient of the award. Those who win these awards never fail to appreciate how special they are.

FUN AND OTHER SPECIALIZED RINGS

From time to time, you will be entering a show that has additional specialized rings. They all usually have several of the following characteristics in common: they are optional; they are largely aimed at entertaining and educating the spectators; they may be conducted by other than fully licensed judges and they may not carry with them additional points in the federation.

One type of ring is known as the "fun" ring. Usually this is a competition among the Household Pet cats and kittens for awards and recognition from the sponsoring club only. These may be for the best cat from the town where the show is held or the "cutest" cat. When they carry an extra admission charge, more often than not they are fund-raisers to help a new club get established or to help a local animal shelter.

Another type of ring is the breed or color "congress." In this, cats of different breeds but similar type (such as all "oriental-type" cats) or cats of similar colors and patterns (such as all tabbies, regardless of breed) are all judged together. Awards are presented to the best cats in each congress.

If the show has additional rings, and you don't understand exactly what they are, contact the Entry Clerk or show manager for more details. And make sure you find out whether there is an additional charge for the ring, and whether your cat will earn any federation points if it participates. That will help you decide if you want to enter.

FEDERATIONS' REGIONAL AND NATIONAL AWARDS

Each federation gives regional and national awards, such as the Best Longhair in the United States, the Best Persian Kitten in the Southeast, or the Second-Best Seal Point Siamese in the United States and Canada. These awards are based on complex scoring systems, which vary substantially from federation to federation and which are subjected to fine-

The Happy Household Pet Cat Club presents rosettes to the Best Cat in many rings at each show.

A Judge's Fancy Award is for the cat "the judge would most like to take home."

tuning from time to time. Essentially, they all put a premium on consistently high performance by a cat (purebred or Household Pet) throughout the show season. The show year for each cat federation is the same: from May 1 to April 30 of the following year.

In seeking titles such as Champion or Companion for your cat, you must keep track of your cat's performance and apply to the federation's office for confirmation of your title.

Regional and national titles and honors from the federations differ. The central office keeps track of the scoring progress of all cats registered with that federation, and, after the end of the season, determines which cats receive what ranking and recognition.

That means you do not need to keep track of your progress in terms of regional or national points, and you do not have to submit documents to be eligible. Your own cat's score, even if you keep it, makes sense only as compared with the scores of all other cats against which it is competing, something you may not be able to determine.

OTHER NATIONAL AWARDS

Besides the major federations, there are several other organizations that present national awards, on the basis of honors won at local cat shows.

Happy Household Pet Cat Club

Unlike the national federations, the Happy Household Pet Cat Club (HHPCC) does not sanction shows to be held by its member clubs. Rather, it permits clubs in all the national federations to award rosettes to Household Pets. However, in return for the rosette, the club must provide HHPCC with a marked catalog from the show. A marked catalog is one that shows all results for all cats. HHPCC uses these catalogs to decide on its own regional and national awards. These awards are given *only* to Household Pet cats that have been registered with HHPCC.

HHPCC's scoring is based only on a combination of your cat's Finals and cats defeated. Finals in an All-Breed ring count more than those in Specialty. The scoring rules provide that the Best Cat in an All-Breed ring receives ten points plus one point for each cat actually defeated. The Second-Best in the All-Breed ring receives nine points, plus one for each cat defeated, and so on down to the Tenth-Best Cat in the All-Breed ring, which receives one point plus one point for each cat defeated.

In the Specialty ring, the Best Cat receives nine points, plus one

The People's Choice is awarded to the most popular cat in the show as chosen by the spectators.

A People's Choice trophy, cape and crown.

for each cat defeated. The Second-Best receives eight plus the number of cats defeated, and so on down through the Ninth-Best, which gets one point plus one point for each cat defeated, as does the Tenth-Best in Specialty.

In some federations, Household Pet cats and kittens are judged together. HHPCC separates the results and awards its points based on cats defeating other cats. Thus, in a CFF show, for example, the "Best Household Pet—All-Breed" may be a kitten, while your adult is Second-Best. Say there are fifty Household Pets, of which fifteen are kittens. Your cat would get ten points (as Best *Cat*) plus thirty-four points for cats (not cats *and* kittens) defeated.

HHPCC also gives points for cats receiving special show-wide awards, such as Best of the Best or King/Queen. The Any Best of the Best (that is, Best of the Best, Second-Best of the Best, and so forth) gets an additional two points, plus one point for each cat it defeated. The cats "defeated" are determined by finding out how many cats were eligible for the award (that is, how many cats received at least one Final award). In the case of King/Queen, two points are given. But there are no additional points for cats defeated.

At the end of the season, each cat's top three shows are added to determine its total points. Back to back shows are counted as two shows. By that, HHPCC means a show that you could enter for either or both days. A single show, held over two days, is counted as one show. HHPCC then determines the top cats in each of its regions and also its national awards.

Kittens are scored separately from adults on the same basis. If they are judged together with the adults, as in CFF, then HHPCC will separate the kittens defeated from the cats, and award its points on the basis of kittens defeated. The points for Finals start at five for a Best Kitten All-Breed, down to one for Fifth- through Tenth-Best. For a Best Kitten in Specialty, the points start at four for Best, and go down to one for Fourth-through Tenth-Best. Just as with adults, cats defeated are added to the Finals points. However, as with the adults, HHPCC counts only your kitten's three best shows for regional and national titles.

The National 9-Lives Morris Award

The 9-Lives National Morris Award competition annually selects the top Household Pet cat in the country. All cats that win local Morris Award trophies from January 1 through December 31 of a given year (not a show year) are eligible to compete in a photo-essay contest. Finalists are then chosen, and the finalists and their owners are then given a trip to California to compete for the national trophy. This is a celebrity-studded, spectacular affair, where the finalists are judged in two categories, beauty (grooming, grace and poise) and personality. The national winner is then chosen and presented with a trophy, in the likeness of Morris the 9-Lives Cat, along with a year's supply of 9-Lives cat food.

Breed Associations' National Awards

Typically, the breed associations tie the awards at the individual federation shows to a system of national and regional recognition and awards. The systems the groups use vary widely, but they are all similar to the systems used by the federations. In fact, they are often keyed to the points awarded by the federations. For example, the Japanese Bobtails Breeders Society scores its top cats by counting one point for each cat (of any breed) that a member's cat defeats in any Final. There is no limit on the number of Finals that can be counted from all federations.

11

Claiming Your Points and Titles

THERE ARE THREE basic points to keep in mind when claiming your points and titles:

- Make sure your cat is registered in the federation so you can claim the title.
- Make sure you know when you can *and must* claim a title.
- Make sure you have your paperwork *complete and readable.*

In every federation, you should file for the title of Champion (or its equivalent for Household Pets) as soon as you can. In those federations where Champions are judged separately against Champions, you *must* file for that title before you attend your next show, and you must use that title at the next show.

The same is not true for the higher titles — that is, you do not have to file right away. However, in those federations in which you have Grand Champions (or the equivalent Household Pet titles) competing against each other, you have to use the correct title for your cat in the first show in which it is eligible to use it.

In general, you can file for the title of Champion (or Grand Champion) after you get back from the weekend. But there is one *important* exception. If you are at a back-to-back show over a weekend (that is two separate shows on two days), you may have a different situation. In ACFA, for example, those cats which have made a Championship (or Grand Championship) on, say, Saturday, must file for that title that day,

THE CAT FANCIERS' ASSOCIATION, INC.
World's Largest Pedigreed Cat Registry
OFFICIAL CHAMPIONSHIP/PREMIERSHIP CLAIM FORM

Request for Championship or Premiership confirmation must be submitted on the official CFA Claim Form or facsimile thereof, and must be mailed to the CFA Office before the opening day of the next show in which the cat is entered. Winners will not be counted if the cat has not been entered under its *exact* registered name, registered ownership, and in the correct class. The cat's CFA registration number must be *printed* in the catalog. Complete the form below and send with the confirmation fee of $3.00 to the CFA Central Office, Department C, 1309 Allaire Avenue, Ocean, NJ 07712.

Registration # _____   Championship ☐   Premiership ☐   (please check one)

Name of Cat _____

Name of Owner _____

Street Address _____

City _____   State _____   Zip _____

DATE	NAME OF SHOW AND LOCATION	JUDGE

300/9-88

A form from CFA used to request confirmation of Championship or Premiership wins.

ACFA REGISTERED NAME:

ACFA REGISTRATION NUMBER: SEX: BIRTHDATE:

NAME OF CLUB	SHOW DATE	ENTRY NO.

PLEASE CHECK THE CONFIRMATION(S) YOU ARE APPLYING FOR:

CHAMPIONSHIP:	CHAMPION ☐	GRAND ☐	HHP:	ROYAL ☐	DOUBLE SUPREME ☐
	DOUBLE CHAMPION ☐	DOUBLE GRAND ☐		DOUBLE ROYAL ☐	TRIPLE SUPREME ☐
	TRIPLE CHAMPION ☐	TRIPLE GRAND ☐		TRIPLE ROYAL ☐	QUAD SUPREME ☐
	QUAD CHAMPION ☐	QUAD GRAND ☐		SUPREME ☐	ROLL OF HONOR ☐

FEES: CONFIRMATION (each) $2.00
    registered w/ACFA

BREEDER:_____

OWNER:_____

CONFIRMATION (each) $4.00
    not registered w/ACFA

ADDRESS:_____

CERTIFICATE OF FRAMING $5.00

TRANSFER OF WINS (each) $20.00

NOTE: CONFIRMATIONS ARE CONFIRMED ONLY UPON WRITTEN REQUEST.

ACFA CONFIRMATION FORM

P.O. BOX 203   PT. LOOKOUT, MO 65726   417-334-5430

A form from ACFA used to request confirmation of wins at a show.   © *1989.*

and then those cats are judged in the Sunday show under their new title. You will hear an announcement to the effect that those cats that achieved Championship or Grand Championship at the Saturday show must file a confirmation form and the appropriate fee, usually with the master clerk or at the announcer's table, *before leaving the showhall on Saturday*. At that point, you are considered to have filed for confirmation, and can use your cat's new title. (Congratulations!)

Of course, this means that you must already know how close your cat is to the title and what paperwork you need to complete.

All paperwork for titles is keyed to your entry in the official show catalog. This is why it is critical that your entry in the catalog be precisely correct, at least in the official version of the show catalog sent to headquarters. If it is not, it may take longer for you to get confirmed, or it may even be impossible for you to get confirmed. If you need a confirmation form, usually there is a current one included in the show catalog.

Here, we will briefly cover two typical types of confirmation forms: ACFA's and TICA's. The former is very simple; the latter substantially more complex. In each case, one tip many exhibitors will give you is to complete one of these forms *before* you get to the show, including on it all the information you need, and then fill it in as the show goes on. That way, you can tell when you are ready to claim a title.

The ACFA form requires your cat's complete and correct *ACFA* registered name and registration number. You also have to include its sex and birth date. These help the federation office double-check that you get all of the points you are claiming.

You must list the name of each club where your cat earned a winner's ribbon or points (as the case may be) toward the title you are claiming. You must also list the dates of the show in which you earned points. So, if your cat won a winner's ribbon on Sunday, July 2, 1989, but not on Saturday, July 1, 1989, at the same show, you list only July 2, 1989.

Notice also that you *must* include the entry number your cat had at the show. Do not guess about this. Keep track.

Then you check off the title you are applying for, include the specified fee, and complete the information on breeder and owner. Of course, if you have an HHP from a shelter, the breeder is "unknown."

You are done.

TICA's confirmation form is more complex, requiring you to keep track of every *time* your cat earns points toward a title. It is very important to make sure that your answers are readable, as the form may be a little cramped.

First, fill out the name of your cat, *as it is registered in TICA*, as

THE INTERNATIONAL CAT ASSOCIATION
APPLICATION FOR RECOGNITION OF WINS

CAT MUST BE TICA REGISTERED

SECTION A:

Date: _____

Name of Cat: _____ TICA Reg. #: _____

Breed: _____ Color: _____ Date of Birth: _____

Sex: _____

Alter: Yes: _____ No: _____

SECTION B:

This cat is already confirmed in TICA as: _____

Application for this cat is being made for the title of:

☐ CH   ☐ GR   ☐ DB GR   ☐ TR GR   ☐ QD GR   ☐ SUP GR
☐ HHP-MASTER   ☐ GR MS   ☐ DB GR MS   ☐ TR GR MS   ☐ QD GR MS   ☐ SUP GR MS

This application ☐ does ☐ does not include wins or championships from other associations to be confirmed.

SECTION C:

	ASSN	NAME OF CLUB	DATE OF SHOW	NAME OF JUDGE	AB OR SP	CAT ENTRY NO.	BOC 1-5	BOD 1-3	FINALS	TOTAL POINTS WON
1										
2										
3										
4										
5										
6										
7										
8										
9										
10										
11										
12										
13										
14										
15										

Total: _____

(BOC) Best of Color Class (SP or AB)

1	2	3	4	5
25	20	15	10	5

(BOD) Best of Division (SP or AB)

1	2	3	NO ADDITIONAL POINTS FOR BREED WINS
25	20	15	

Allbreed Show Finals

1	2	3	4	5	6	7	8	9	10
200	190	180	170	160	150	140	130	120	110

Specialty Show Finals

1	2	3	4	5	6	7	8	9	10
150	140	130	120	110	100	90	80	70	60

CHAMPION	HOUSEHOLD PET	REQUIREMENTS FOR TITLES
Champion	Master	300 points from 4 different judges, plus one final
GR CH	GR MS	1000 points with 6 finals from 4 different judges — 3 in Top 5 SP or Top 10 AB
DB GR	DB GR MS	2000 points plus 1 final in either format as a GR
TR GR	TR GR MS	3000 points plus 1 final in either format as a DB GR
QD GR	QD GR MS	4000 points plus 1 final in either format as a TR GR
SUP GR	SUP GR MS	6000 points plus 1 Best Cat as a QD GR

SECTION D:

I hereby certify that the foregoing is a true and correct list of the wins and points won by this cat.

_____
Owner's Signature

_____
Owner's Address

FORM C-1040 (05/01/87)

A form from TICA used to apply for recognition of wins at a show. © *1989.*

well as its registration number. Then provide the breed (spelled out). Household Pet is a "breed" for this purpose. Provide the color under which your cat has been judged and is registered. Provide its date of birth and its sex and indicate if it has been altered. These items permit the TICA office to double-check the accuracy of the points you have claimed, as well as your cat's eligibility for a particular title.

If your cat has already been confirmed in TICA for a title, include it. If you know it, also include the number of points you have already claimed to get that title. Then check off the title you are claiming. The top line of titles are for Championship and Alter class cats; the lower line is for HHPs. Remember, you do not include all of the wins and points it took to get that *original* title; only list those which are going toward the title you are claiming.

Then, you must specifically indicate if you are claiming wins or Championships from another federation. (As we have mentioned, whether you can do this, and under what circumstances, varies from federation to federation and over time). Before you do this, check with the TICA office on whether you can do this, for what titles and at what additional cost.

In Section C of the TICA Form, provide a list of the judgings involved in your application for a title. Each of these is taken from the show catalog of the show involved. Provide the name of the association sponsoring the show involved in the first column. In the second, provide the name of the club. In the third column, provide the date on which the judging occurred. In the fourth, give the name of the judge. Abbreviating the first name and giving the last name is enough.

In the fifth column, indicate if the judging was All-Breed (AB) or Specialty (SP). In the sixth column, give your cat's entry number for that show. In the seventh column, indicate what placing your cat received in terms of Best of Color Class (BOC)—1–5 or not awarded (n/a). In the eighth column, do the same for the results in Best of Division (BOD)—1–3 or not awarded (n/a). In the ninth column, list the Final your cat was awarded (1–10) or not awarded (n/a). Please make sure that you fill out *every item* for each set of points you claim.

In the last column, put the total number of points you are claiming from the judging you have just described. To help you, TICA has provided a key below the table. TICA has also provided a summary of the points you need to claim each title. But remember, if there were fewer than twenty-five cats judged in a ring and you are claiming points from the Finals, only the *five top* Finals placings carry points.

185

Now, add up the points you have claimed on this form, sign it and mail it in. You will find information about the required fee included in the show catalog.

You are done.

12

Travel and Accommodations

FOR YOUR SAFETY and for the safety of your cat, always travel with your cat in a travel cage, also called a carrier. There are many types of carriers, ranging from cardboard carriers to molded plastic carriers with either metal or plastic fixtures and fastenings. Cat carriers are not too expensive, and they are made by several different companies, so you have a choice when you buy one.

Different carriers have different features, some of which may be important to you. Some even have wheels and a handle for pulling the carrier. Since you will be keeping it in the showhall, make sure the carrier you use can be washed and disinfected. The plastic carriers all disassemble easily and can be soaked in a sink or bathtub.

Make sure you buy the proper size carrier. Travel cages come in many different sizes, some small enough for a kitten, others able to accommodate a large cat, like a Maine Coon, in comfort. You don't want your cat to feel cramped in the carrier, so make certain it is big enough for the cat as an adult and as a kitten.

Most cat carriers are approved for air transportation in the cargo area of an airplane. Be sure you check with the airline you will be using regarding the specific model you have.

If you want your cat in the cabin with you, you will have to make prior, special arrangements with the airline you will be using. Also, make sure your carrier is made to fit *under* the airplane seat. There are two cages in common use for this type of travel. One is a molded plastic carrier that is low enough to fit with ease under an airplane seat. The

187

Many cat show exhibitors show their breed, their cattery name or just their love for cats on their license plates.

If you are on the road at 5:00 A.M. on a Saturday or Sunday and see a van or car ahead of you with this sign in the window, follow that van and you will find yourself at a cat show.

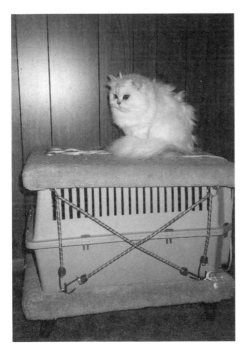

Champion Alrene Kali's Private Dancer ("Fancy") on top of a travel cage that has been adapted for use as a grooming table also.

other is a soft-sided carrier that looks something like a ladies' handbag and is carried that way. This is very comfortable if you are dealing with major airports and have a long walk in the airline terminal.

When outfitting your travel carrier, keep in mind the season of the year as well as the comfort of your cat. The bottom of the carrier can be cushioned with a soft blanket, lambswool or a towel. Most travel cages will easily accommodate a soft-sided cat bed.

If the weather is cold, or if your cat feels more secure not being able to see outside the cage, the cage can easily be covered. Many vendors at cat shows carry travel cage covers. These are made to fit the various sizes of carrying cages and will accommodate the cage handle. If you don't have a cage cover made especially for the cage, you can cover the outside with a towel, folded sheet or pillowcase, secured with alligator clips.

In hot weather, be very careful of leaving empty travel cages in your car during the show. They can get hot to the point that they must cool down before you can safely put your cat in the carrier. If you must leave the travel cage in the car during a show, bring it into the showhall at least an hour before you are ready to leave so that it can cool down. Breaking it apart often helps it to cool down faster.

For driving short distances, a regular cat travel carrier is adequate. But if you will be driving for several hours, you might consider getting a bigger, metal cage that stays in the car, holds a litterbox and provides room for your cat to move around. Then, when you arrive at the show, you can transfer your cat from the cage to the carrier. But, *be careful!* When transferring a cat between carrier and car cage, always do so with *all* the car doors and windows closed. Otherwise, your cat may attempt to escape and run into the street. Also, don't forget that the cage you leave in the car during the show can get very hot (or cold). Make sure it is comfortable before your cat gets into it again.

For tips and other information on shipping pets, particularly outside of the United States, order the most current edition of *Traveling With Your Pet*, compiled and printed by the American Society for the Prevention of Cruelty to Animals, 441 East 92nd Street, New York, New York 10128.

GETTING YOUR CAT USED TO THE SHOW HOTEL

When a show is being set up, the show committee contacts hotels or motels near the showhall that will let the cats stay with their owners in the rooms. You can usually find out which hotels do this from the show flyer or the confirmation. If not, call the show manager for help—but call well in advance of the show.

Staying in the hotel is generally fun for cats going to shows. Even if your cat has never stayed in a hotel before, you will find that its natural curiosity makes the experience fun for the cat. But before your cat starts to enjoy exploring the hotel room, you will have to do some exploring of your own. Before you let your cat out of the carrier, do all of the following to "catproof" the room:

1. Check all windows and doors and make sure they are securely locked.
2. Check under the bed. This is the area that will generally be the dirtiest and, of course, will be the first place that is attractive to your cat. Pick up any trash you may find under the bed and dispose of it. Check the bottom of the mattress. Sometimes there will be a hole in the mattress that your cat can crawl into. This is also true of beds that are on a platform. If the mattress is torn, the cat can get inside the mattress and inside the platform. If you move the mattress and check inside the platform, you may find all kinds of trash that can endanger your cat. Unfortunately, this happens in the "best" hotels. You may have to ask for another room if the situation is too dangerous.
3. Check the other furniture in the room. Cats can get into places that humans don't know exist. Make sure you can reach your cat wherever it hides and try to spot all the likely hiding places. Many hotel dressers are open at the bottom, allowing your cat to jump up inside the furniture. If your cat seems to have "disappeared," it might very well have found the secret entrance into the dresser.
4. Check the carpet for insects and fleas. This is very important. If you have any suspicion that your cat may pick up fleas from the carpet in a hotel, use a flea collar and consider washing the cat with a flea shampoo upon your return home. When your cat is wearing a flea collar, look for signs that your cat may be allergic to the chemicals in the collar.
5. One of the easiest ways to make sure that your belongings don't get turned into cat toys is to keep everything in drawers. Otherwise, you may be hunting all over the floor and under the beds for something like your contact lens case.
6. Bring your own "Do Not Disturb" sign and use it whenever you are out of the room, even if it is "just for a moment."

Some kittens travel more comfortably in a sweater. It also helps keep them warm while they are being transported from the car to the showhall.

Two cat travel cages can be stacked on a wheeled luggage cart for easy transport.

If you find that the room you have in the hotel is dirty or otherwise unsatisfactory, don't hesitate to have the room changed. Whether or not you are getting a special rate, you are paying for a clean, safe hotel room and you should get it. Don't forget to let the show committee know if you have real problems with the show hotel. They need to know this so they can choose a different hotel for their next show.

After you have checked out the hotel room, set up the litterbox your cat will be using. At that point, remove your cat from the carrier and place it *immediately* in the box. If you have set the box up in the bathroom (which is usually the best place), you may want to close the door for a couple of minutes. After seeing the box and exploring the bathroom, your cat will be ready to explore the rest of the hotel room. Once somewhat settled, the cat might like being fed. This is generally a good time for you to go out for dinner yourself. When you are out of the room, remember to put the "Do Not Disturb" sign on the door.

If you find that your cat cannot get used to the hotel room or appears very nervous, you might want to use a cage. This is also true if you have a male who sprays. For this reason you might consider buying a medium-sized cage or bringing the car cage, if you have used one, into the hotel room. Metal cages usually are easily collapsed and lightweight. If you get one that is about twenty-four by twenty-four inches, it will hold a small litter pan as well as a small cat bed. This is a good size for a small-to medium-sized cat. If you have to cage your cat overnight, as well as in the showhall, be sure to allow it some time to get out of the cage for exercise as well as play time with you.

HOW TO KEEP THE SHOW HOTEL CLEAN

Many hotels do not accept pets in the rooms because they have had bad experiences with pets. If a cat sprays or otherwise soils the carpet, the odor can be extremely difficult to remove and can occasionally make the room impossible to rent to other people. If a hotel has trouble with exhibitors leaving dirty rooms, it may not permit cats to be housed in the hotel in the future. That may affect the ability of cat clubs to hold shows in a given area. Also, since many clubs use a hall in the show hotel as the showhall, a potential showhall site may also be eliminated if the exhibitors do not keep the hotel rooms clean. For all of these reasons, it is critical that the hotel room be left clean and odor-free when you check out.

Here are some hints:

1. Use disposable litter pans lined with a plastic litter liner. If you are staying only one night, put the litter for the pan in the liner at home, and then close it with a twist-tie. Then, line the litter pan with the prefilled bag when you get into the room.
2. Bring your own large plastic trash bag for litter and trash disposal. In the morning, gather up the litter liner, with the used litter in it, and seal it with a twist-tie. Dispose of the litter and the liner in the plastic trash bag, along with any leftover cat food, and seal that bag with a twist-tie. This bag can be left in the bathroom by the wastebasket, outside the door or in the rubbish bin, depending upon the instructions the hotel or the show committee may have given you. Never dispose of cat litter by attempting to flush it down the toilet.
3. If your cat has an accident, you must be prepared to clean it up with your own supplies. For this reason, pack paper towels, soap and a deodorizer. Dispose of the paper towels in the trash bag you are using for litter disposal. *Never* use the hotel towels for cleaning up.
4. Bring a solid room deodorizer with you and leave it in the room with the litterbox. This can help eliminate odors.

Many show flyers suggest you confine your cat in the hotel bathroom when the cat is in the hotel room. This can be very unfair to the cat, which has already been confined to cages during the show and while traveling. The bathroom can also be a dangerous place for a young kitten as the surfaces of the sink, vanity and bathtub are slick and provide little traction for the cat's paws. You should consider confining your cat to the cage or to the bathroom if you are out of the hotel room for a brief period of time. But when you are there, and you can supervise, your cat should be able to move around the room and get some exercise.

AFTER THE SHOW

That the show is over doesn't mean your work has ended. There is as much to do after the show as there is preparing for it. This is the time you must disinfect everything you took to the show. Since this helps to protect your cat from disease, it is just as important as the precautions you took at the showhall.

Some exhibitors begin disinfecting as soon as they get home. If you cannot do this, place all the cat equipment in a separate, closed room. Place all washable clothes, cage curtains, cage cover and so forth in a laundry hamper or trash can lined with a plastic trash bag. Secure the bag with a twist-tie and seal the hamper. Keep this in the same room with the contaminated show equipment. Make sure your cats and any other pets cannot get into this room. You don't want to infect any of your animals with something you may have accidentally picked up at a cat show.

We suggest the following disinfecting procedure:

1. Wash the cage curtains, benching cage floor covering, cat bed and anything else washable used in or on the benching cage in hot water, soap, a disinfectant (such as Nolvasan or laundry bleach) and a deodorizer. Rinse thoroughly and dry.
2. Disassemble the travel cage. Wash the travel cage with hot water and a disinfectant. Wash a second time with hot water and a deodorizer. Dry thoroughly and reassemble.
3. Wash all food dishes, water dishes and anything else you brought into the showhall with hot water and a disinfectant.
4. Wash all your clothes separately from your regular laundry, using a disinfectant.
5. Clean your shoes. Don't forget to use a disinfectant on the soles of the shoes. If you wore washable shoes, wash them with a disinfectant.
6. If you feel you may have exposed your cat to fleas or a fungus such as ringworm, immediately bathe the cat with a shampoo made for this purpose.

Some exhibitors routinely isolate the cats they have shown for at least twenty-four hours. If this is impossible, be certain you watch the cat carefully for any signs of infectious disease, fleas or fungus.

However, just because we have stressed being very cautious, don't get the impression that showing your cat is endangering its health. These are just routine precautions. While you know how well you care for your cat, you can't assume that everyone at the show also takes such excellent care of their cats. Also, you are in a showhall, usually overheated, with fifty to two hundred other exhibitors and possibly thousands of spectators. Colds and flus are easily passed from one exhibitor to another or from spectators to exhibitors. For these reasons, a thorough disinfecting procedure is important. It really doesn't take much time, and it helps protect the health of your cat.

Glossary

ACA: American Cat Association, a cat federation.

ACFA: The American Cat Fanciers Association, Inc., a cat federation.

ADULT: For purposes of cat shows, a cat that is at least eight months old at the time of the show.

AGENT: A person other than a cat's registered owner who brings a cat to a show and handles it. The person handling the cat is the "agent" and must be listed in the show entry form. The agent is fully responsible for the cat while at the show and is generally treated like the owner.

ALL-BREED JUDGE: A judge who is licensed to judge an All-Breed ring. An All-Breed judge may also judge as a Specialty judge.

ALL-BREED RING: A ring where longhair cats and shorthair cats are judged against each other.

ALTER: A class in which spayed and neutered cats are judged. (See Premier.) A cat that has been surgically corrected to prevent breeding.

BACK-TO-BACK JUDGING: A show over two or more days in which the same person judges cats more than once. Usually the person will judge one day as an All-Breed judge and the other as a Specialty judge.

BACK-TO-BACK SHOWS: Two or more shows held at the same place on consecutive days, sanctioned by the same federation. Each day is treated as a separate show.

BENCH: This term refers to the place that your cat is assigned in the showhall. It also is used to refer to a benched cat.

BENCHED CAT: A cat that is present and qualified for competition at a cat show.

BEST OF THE BEST: An award given at the end of a cat show to the cat, kitten, Alter, Premier, Household Pet cat and Household Pet kitten that scored highest during the entire show.

BOB: Best of Breed.

BOC: Best of Color or Best of Class.

BOD: Best of Division.

BREED STANDARDS: Those standards formulated by a cat federation for use in judging a particular breed. These standards are the ideal for that breed.

C. or CH.: Champion.

CAT FANCY: A synonym for a cat federation.

CAT FEDERATION: An association of persons and clubs involved in breeding, showing and judging cats. Among its activities are sanctioning shows and registering cats.

CAT: A feline, of either sex, over eight months of age.

CATALOG: The official record of all cats entered in a particular show.

CATTERY: A name registered by a cat breeder to identify the line of breeding. A registered cattery name always appears as a prefix to the name of a cat bred by that cattery-breeder.

CD: Closing date.

CFA: The Cat Fanciers' Association, Inc., a cat federation.

CFF: Cat Fanciers' Federation, Inc., a cat federation.

CLASSIFICATION CALL: An announcement to all those showing HHPs at a show to bring their cats to a designated ring, before the judging. The purpose is to make sure that the HHPs have been properly classified for judging purposes. Usually only done in TICA shows.

CLERK: This usually refers to a ring clerk.

CLOSING DATE: The date by which you must have entered to be able to show your cat at a specific event.

CONFIRM: This term most often means receiving an acknowledgment (''confirmation'') that your cat has been entered in a show. It can also refer to the need to file a ''confirmation'' to obtain a title for your cat.

CONFORMATION: Sometimes used in describing a cat; a comment about its ''conformation,'' that is, about its structure or how it conforms to the Standard for its breed.

DAM: The mother of a cat.

DB. GR. or DGC.: Double Grand Champion.

DB. GR. MS. or DGM.: Double Grand Master.

DECLAW: To have the claws from the paws of a cat permanently removed, usually by surgery. The only declawed cats that can be shown in cat shows are HHPs, and not every show or federation allows declawed HHPs to be shown.

DISTINGUISHED MERIT: A recognition granted by CFA to a cat that has produced a specific number of offspring that have achieved certain titles. Similar recognition is given by other federations.

DM: Distinguished Merit.

EARLY BIRD ENTRY: An entry date before the closing date. Early bird entries come in at lower prices per cat.

EBCD: Early bird closing date. The closing date for an early bird entry.

EBEF: Early bird entry fee.

EC: Entry Clerk.

ENTRY CLERK: The club official responsible for receiving, processing and confirming all entries to a show. This may also be a commercial service hired by the club.

ENTRY FORM: The form used by a cat club that provides the information necessary to enter a cat show.

EOR: Benching at the end of a row.

EXHIBITOR: A person who is showing (exhibiting) a cat in a show.

FEDERATION: See Cat Federation.

FINAL or FINALING: Being called up at the end of judging to receive a ''Best'' award.

FLAT: A colored indicator of what awards (such as winner's ribbon and merit award, as well as Best, Second-Best and so forth, of color, class, division and breed) a judge has given a cat. They are put on top of the cat's judging cage while the cat is in it.

FLYER: See Show Flyer.

GENETIC CODE: A combination of letters and numbers designed to describe a cat in genetic terms. The purpose is to permit the cat to be classified properly for show and breeding purposes.

GR., GRC. or GCH.: Grand Champion.

GR. MS., GM., or GRM.: Grand Master.

GROOMING CALL: A polite warning to exhibitors to prepare their cats for judging in the very near future.

HEAD RING CLERK: See Ring Clerk.

HHP: Household Pet.

HOUSEHOLD PET: A nonpedigreed cat or kitten or a pedigreed cat or kitten being exhibited in a class with nonpedigreed cats or kitten. Some cat federations have a separate procedure for registering Household Pets. Some federations also permit Household Pets to earn titles equivalent to those won by pedigreed cats. Household Pets are usually required to be altered by a certain age and may or may not be permitted to be declawed.

JUDGE: An individual who is licensed by a cat federation to judge in its shows.

K. or KIT.: Kitten.

KITTEN: A feline, of either sex, under the age of eight months. For show purposes, a cat that is at least four months old, but less than eight months old. Its age is measured on the day of the show.

LH.: Longhair.

LITTER: All of the kittens born of the same sire and dam at the same time.

LITTER REGISTRATION: The recording by a cat federation of the birth of a litter, giving the date of birth, number of kittens, sire and dam. Litter applications are submitted by the breeder of the litter.

LONGHAIR: One of the two groups into which all cats are divided.

M., MS. or MAS.: Master.

MARKED CATALOG: A written record of all the decisions of all the judges in a show. It is prepared by the master clerk on a corrected copy of the show catalog.

MASTER CLERK: An individual responsible for keeping track of all the judging decisions made in the show.

NBC: New Breed or Color.

NEU.: Neuter.

NEUTER: A male cat who has been castrated to prevent breeding.

NONVETTED SHOW: A show at which the cats are *not* examined by a veterinarian before they are brought into the hall or judged.

NOV.: Novice.

NW: National Winner. A designation used to indicate a cat that has received a national award from CFA.

OPN: Open.

PAPERS: One way to refer to a cat's certificate of registration and pedigree form.

PEDIGREE: A document showing a cat's background for three, four or five generations. A three-generation pedigree is the cat, plus three generations back. A pedigree gives names, colors and registration numbers for each cat in the pedigree. Show titles are usually also given.

PEDIGREED CAT: This usually refers to a cat whose heritage is known, documented and registered.

POSTING: Placing the numbers of the cats called to a Final on top of the judging cage.

PREMIER: A class in which altered cats are judged.

PROVISIONAL: A class of cats judged separately at a cat show. Usually, the breed or type of cat has not yet been accepted for full competition purposes, but is being shown and measured against a provisional written Standard.

QD. GR. or QGC.: Quadruple Grand Champion.

QD. GR. MS. or QGM.: Quadruple Grand Master.

QUEEN: A breeding female cat.

REGISTERED CAT: A cat (whether purebred or HHP) that has completed the requirements for registration with one of the cat federations.

REGISTRATION: The initial recording of a cat's individual cat name and owner record in a cat federation. This also refers to the registration certificate issued by a cat federation to the registered owner of the cat.

REGISTRATION NUMBER: A unique number assigned by a federation to identify one cat. Each federation issues its own set of registration numbers.

REGISTRATION RULES: The rules and guidelines set up by a cat federation for the registration of cats, litters, catteries and so forth.

REGISTRY: One term used to describe a cat federation, taken from one of its primary roles, registering the birth and pedigree of cats.

RING: A competition judged by one judge.

RING CLERK: An individual responsible for keeping track of all decisions by a particular judge in one ring, as well as assisting the judge in managing the ring.

RING STEWARD: An individual assisting the judge and ring clerk. Usually responsible for cleaning the judging cages after each cat has been removed.

ROSETTE: An award, usually for a Final.

SCORER: An individual responsible for seeing that the results of shows in a given federation are correctly tabulated.

SH.: Shorthair.

SHORTHAIR: One of the two groups into which all cats are divided.

SHOW: A series of rings of judging sponsored by a cat club.

SHOW CATALOG: See Catalog.

SHOW COMMITTEE: A group of members of a club sponsoring a show. It is usually made up of the Entry Clerk, the show manager and one or more members of the club. It is responsible for setting up the show, hiring the judges and making sure the show runs smoothly.

SHOW CONFIRMATION: A form used by a cat club confirming your entry into a show.

SHOW FLYER: This contains essential information about a show, including judges and fees.

SHOW MANAGER: A member of the club sponsoring the show who is primarily responsible for seeing that the show runs smoothly.

SHOW RULES: Rules formulated by a specific cat federation governing all the aspects of how that federation's show is to be managed.

SHOW SEASON: The period from May 1 to April 30 of the following year.

SIRE: The father of a cat.

SPAY: A female cat who has had a hysterectomy to prevent breeding and heat cycles.

SPECIALTY JUDGE: A judge who is licensed to judge a Specialty ring. The judge may be licensed to judge a shorthair ring, a longhair ring, or both, but is not licensed to judge an All-Breed ring.

SPECIALTY RING: A ring in which only cats of the same hair length (longhair or shorthair) are judged against each other.

SPECTATOR: Someone who attends a cat show, but is not an exhibitor.

SPRAYING: A male cat's habit of urinating anywhere, probably associated with establishing territory.

SPY: Spay.

STANDARDS OF PERFECTION: Another name for breed Standards. Often just referred to as "Standards."

STEWARD: See Ring Steward.

STUD CAT: A breeding male cat.

SUP. GR. or SGC.: Supreme Grand Champion.

SUP. GR. MS. or SGM.: Supreme Grand Master.

THIRD CALL: This is the last call to bring a cat or kitten to the ring. Usually it is given as "third and final call," with a warning that any cat not brought to the ring within a specified period of time will be marked absent.

TICA: The International Cat Association, Inc., a cat federation.

TOP FIVE FORMAT: A Final in which only the top five cats (kittens, Alter/Premiers, HHPs) are recognized and receive points.

TOP TEN FORMAT: A Final in which the top ten cats (kittens, Alter/Premiers, HHPs) are recognized and receive points.

TR. GR. or TGC.: Triple Grand Champion.

TR. GR. MS. or TGM.: Triple Grand Master.

UCF: United Cat Fanciers, a cat federation.

VETTED SHOW: A show at which the cats are examined by a veterinarian either before they are brought into the hall or before they are judged. (See Nonvetted Show.)

WHOLE MALE: A male cat that has not been neutered.

A Handy Guide to Four Federations' Titles

Pedigreed	*ACFA*	*CFA*	*CFF*	*TICA*
Kittens	No titles	No titles	No titles	No titles
Cats	Do not have to Final to Champion	Do not have to Final to Champion	Do not have to Final to Champion	Must Final to Champion

	Titles:
	  Champion
	  Double Ch.
	  Triple Ch.
	  Quadruple
	    Ch.
	  Grand Ch.
	  Double Gr.
	  Triple Gr.
	  Quadruple
	    Gr.
		Titles:
		  Champion
		
		Grand Ch.
			Titles:
			  Champion
			
			Grand Ch.
			Master Gr.
				Titles:
				  Champion
				
				Grand Ch.
				Double Gr.
				Triple Gr.
				Quadruple
				  Gr.
				Supreme
				  Gr.

Alters	Titles:
	  "Spay" or
	  "Neuter"
	  Champion,
	  etc.
		Titles:
		  Premier,
		  Grand
		  Premier
			Titles:
			  "Altered"
			  Champion,
			  etc.
				Same Titles as cats

FEDERATION

Household Pets (HHPs)	ACFA	CFA	CFF	TICA
Kittens	No titles	No titles	No titles	No titles
	Compete with HHPs (adults)	Compete with HHPs (adults)	Compete with HHPs (adults)	Compete with other kittens
Adults	Titles: Royal Double Royal Triple Royal Supreme Double Sup. Triple Sup. Quadruple Supreme	No titles	Titles: Companion Grand Companion Master Grand Companion	Titles parallel to cats: Master Grand Master Double GRM Triple GRM Quadruple GRM Supreme GRM
	Kittens compete with adults	Kittens compete with adults	Kittens compete with adults	Adults do not compete with kittens
	HHPs compete in All-Breed and Specialty rings	HHPs compete in All-Breed and Specialty rings	HHPs compete only in All-Breed rings	HHPs compete in All-Breed and Specialty rings

APPENDIX I

Keeping Score in ACFA

PUREBRED KITTENS

All purebred kittens are divided into males and females. They are then assigned to one of several color classes. In each class (that is, cats of the same color, pattern and sex) the judge awards first-, second- and third-place ribbons. In larger classes, fourth and fifth places may be awarded.

The judge also awards a Best of Color and Second-Best of Color to the best two cats among *all* of the cats of the same color variety, regardless of sex (that is, males and females compete against each other). Next, the judge awards Best Kitten and Second-Best Kitten from among all kittens of the *same breed* (including all colors).

Kittens are then judged for Best Kitten, Second-Best Kitten, and so forth from *all breeds*. In each ring in an ACFA show, the judge will present the awards for the top five kittens in the specialty rings (longhair and shorthair) and to the top ten in the All-Breed rings.

Kittens do not compete for titles such as Champion or Grand Champion. Neutered and spayed kittens may not compete in the kitten class.

CHAMPIONSHIP CATS AND ALTERS

Initially, all adult purebred cats and Alters are assigned to the Championship class, which is in turn divided into several "classes." Each class is made up of cats of the same sex and color, with the same status in competition. For example, a Blue Point Siamese cat may be in any one of the following six classes:

- Male Open (for non-Champions)
- Male Champion
- Male Grand Champion
- Female Open (for non-Champions)
- Female Champion
- Female Grand Champion

Titles for Alters and "whole or entire" cats are the same, except that the word Spay (for a female Alter) or Neuter (for a male Alter) is added to the title. Alters are judged the same way cats are.

All cats (and Alters) start off as "Opens," that is non-Champions. In each class, the judge awards first-, second- and third-place ribbons. In larger classes, a fourth and fifth place may be awarded.

The judge then awards a winner's ribbon to the Best Open Male in each color and to the Best Open Female in each color.

The judge also awards a Best of Color and Second-Best of Color to the best two cats among *all* of the cats of the same color, regardless of sex and class (that is, Opens, Champions and Grand Champions of the same color compete against each other). From there, the judge awards Best of Breed and Second-Best of Breed from among all cats of the same breed (but of *any* color).

ACFA requires that Best of Breed and Second-Best of Breed go *only* to cats that have won a Best of Color or Second-Best of Color. The judge also awards the Best and Second-Best Open, Champion and Grand Champion.

To become a Champion in ACFA, your cat must receive at least four winner's ribbons in the same color class from at least four different judges. At that point, you should immediately apply to have your cat confirmed as a Champion. You may be able to do that at the end of the first day of a show.

Once your cat is a Champion, you must compete in the Champion class, not the Open class. Here, the judge compares all Champions in the same class (including Double, Triple and Quadruple Champions), and the Best Champion Male and the Best Champion Female in each color class earns a Champion winner's ribbon.

In each ring, the judge will present the awards for the top five Alters or cats in the Specialty (shorthair or longhair) rings, and to the top ten in the All-Breed rings.

In a Specialty ring, the judge will present awards for the Best Grand

Champion, Second-Best Grand Champion, Best Champion and Second-Best Champion. In the All-Breed ring, the judge will also announce the Best and Second-Best Grand Champions.

At this point, you are competing for multiple Championships. After your cat becomes a Champion, it must earn four more *Champion winner's* ribbons to become a Double Champion, eight more to become a Triple Champion, and twelve more to become a Quadruple Champion. To achieve the status of Quadruple Champion, the last four Champion winner's ribbons must have been awarded by four different judges.

At this point, you have to file immediately for status as Quadruple Champion.

ACFA, unlike most other federations, will allow you to use winner's ribbons won in other federations toward its titles, but only under very strict conditions. First, your cat must already have been confirmed as a Champion with ACFA. Second, you can use these winner's ribbons toward the Double and Triple Championships *only*. Third, you have to file a separate application with ACFA to use them and pay a substantial fee for each winner's ribbon you wish to transfer.

From this point on, you are competing for the status of Grand Champion. To become a Grand Champion, your cat must have received at least six Finals, under six different judges, in any combination of All-Breed or Specialty. Two of these must be fifth cat or higher. What is important here is that you can have achieved these Finals while your cat was a Champion or even an Open.

Your cat is now competing for the status of Double, Triple or Quadruple Grand Champion. For each of these, your cat must get thirty "Grand Championship points." You earn these as follows:

- To get any points, you must earn a first place.
- You get one Grand Championship point for each *Grand* Champion your cat defeated.
- You get one additional Grand Championship point for winning Best of Breed or Second-Best of Breed.
- You get two more Grand Championship points for winning Best Cat, Second-Best Cat or Third-Best Cat (in either the All-Breed or Specialty ring). If you get Fourth-Best Cat or Fifth-Best Cat in either ring, you get one Grand Championship point.

You cannot get more than five points in any one ring. When your cat becomes a Quadruple Grand Champion, it will be placed on the ACFA Supreme Roll of Honor.

HOUSEHOLD PET CATS AND KITTENS

In ACFA, all Household Pets above the age of four months are judged together. If the Household Pet cat is eight months old or older, it must be spayed or neutered in order to claim any titles or to receive any year-end awards from ACFA.

They are divided into two groups, longhairs and shorthairs. All cats (and Alters) start off as "Opens." The first step in judging in ACFA is the "Merit" ribbon, which is awarded based on an examination of the cat's health and cleanliness.

In each ring in an ACFA show, the judge will present the awards for the top five Household Pets in the Specialty rings, and to the top ten in the All-Breed rings. The judge also designates the Best and Second-Best Longhair Royal Household Pets, the Best and Second-Best Shorthair Royal Household Pets, the Best and Second-Best Supreme Longhair Household Pets and the Best and Second-Best Supreme Shorthair Household Pets.

However, the judge does not separately designate the Best and Second-Best Royals and Supremes.

The Household Pet cats compete for the titles of "Royal" and "Supreme." To become a Royal in ACFA, your Household Pet cat must earn at least 250 points. To be a Double Royal requires at least 500 points, and a Triple Royal requires at least 750 points.

To attain the title "Supreme" requires a total of 1,000 points. "Double Supreme" requires 1,250 points, "Triple Supreme" requires 1,500 points and "Quadruple Supreme" requires a total of 1,750 points.

Points are earned as follows: In an All-Breed ring, the Best All-Breed HHP gets 50 points, the Second-Best 46 points, the Third-Best 42 points, the Fourth-Best 38 points, the Fifth-Best 34 points, the Sixth-Best 25 points, the Seventh-Best 23 points, the Eighth-Best 21 points, the Ninth-Best 19 points, and the Tenth-Best 17 points.

In a Specialty ring, the Best HHP gets 25 points, the Second-Best 23 points, the Third-Best 21 points, the Fourth-Best 19 points, and the Fifth-Best 17 points. If your cat does not get a Final, but is the Best Longhair *or* Shorthair Royal *or* Supreme, it gets 3 points. If it does not get a Final, but is the Second-Best Longhair *or* Shorthair Royal *or* Supreme, it gets 2 points. You cannot get points for both a Final *and* a Best or Second-Best Royal or Supreme.

When your Household Pet has obtained 2,000 points, you can apply for recognition on the ACFA Household Pet Supreme Roll of Honor.

Colors of Flats

Class

First Place	Dark Blue
Second Place	Red
Third Place	Yellow
Winner	Red, White and Blue
Merit	*

Color

Best	Black
Second-Best	White

Division

Best	*
Second-Best	*

Breed

Best	*
Second-Best	*

Champion

Best	*
Second-Best	*

*No color specified. Typically, it is a color or combination of colors other than one used for another flat.

APPENDIX II

Keeping Score in CFA

PUREBRED KITTENS

The first step for judging a kitten in CFA is for it to be in a "color class," so that it is judged against kittens of the same color and pattern in the same breed. The judge will award first through third place to each kitten in the color class of each sex.

The judge then judges all of the kittens of the same color, *of both sexes*, against each other. From among them, the judge then announces the Best of Color Class and Second-Best of Color Class.

Then the judge reviews all of the shorthair or longhair kittens and awards rosettes in Finals to the top ten kittens. If there are fewer than thirty-five kittens, the judge awards only the "top five" rosettes. If the ring is "All-Breed," then the "top ten" covers both longhair and shorthair kittens.

CHAMPIONSHIP CATS

The first step for judging a cat in CFA is for it to be judged in the "Open" class—that is, with cats that have not yet become Champions. Each cat is placed in a "color class," so it is judged against cats of the same color and pattern, in the same breed and of the same sex. An "Open" is judged with other Open entries.

The judge will award first through third place to each open in the color class. Then, the Best Male Open and the Best Female Open of each color class will each be awarded a winner's ribbon.

An Open that has won six winner's ribbons from at least four different judges is awarded the title of Champion.

The judge then judges all Champions in the color class against each other, and all of the Grand Champions of the color class against each other. From among all of the cats, Opens, Champions and Grand Champions, of both sexes in the *same* color class, the judge then announces the Best of Color Class and Second-Best of Color Class.

Now the judge looks at all of the color classes making up a division, such as solid or tabby, and then awards a Best of Division and a Second-Best of Division. Then the judge considers all of the divisions making up the breed, and selects the Best of Breed and Second-Best of Breed. The judge also awards a Best Champion of Breed or Division from among all the Champions in competition in a given breed.

The judge then reviews all of the shorthair or longhair cats and awards rosettes in Finals to the top ten cats. If the judge is "All-Breed," then the top ten covers both longhair and shorthair adult cats. In the Finals, the judge also awards separate recognition for the Best and Second-Best Champions. If the ring is a Specialty ring—that is, either for long-hairs or shorthairs—the judge recognizes the Best and Second-Best Long-hair (or Shorthair) Champion. In an All-Breed Ring, the judge recognizes *both* the Best and Second-Best Longhair *and* the Best and Second-Best Shorthair Champions, as well as Best Champion and Second-Best Champion. These "best" Champions do not have to be among the judge's ten Finalists. The awards of Best and Second-Best Champion count toward a cat's efforts to achieve a Grand Championship.

Therefore, a cat shown as an Open might win a first and a winner's ribbon, but only receive a Second-Best of Color Class if another cat of the same color, which is already a Grand Champion, defeats it.

Once your cat is a Champion, it then competes to become a Grand Champion. The first step here is to make sure that you have filed for your Championship before the next show. Then, your cat competes in shows as a Champion. To become a Grand Champion, it must collect 200 Grand Championship points under at least three different judges. You collect points as follows: If your cat wins Best Champion in its Breed/Division, it gets 1 Grand Championship point for every benched Champion it defeated in the Breed/Division. A benched Champion is one that is present in the showhall and was judged in at least one ring.

If your cat is called up for Finals as Best Specialty Champion (that is, either longhair *or* shorthair), but does not receive a rosette, it receives 1 Grand Championship point for every benched longhair *or* shorthair

Champion it defeated. If it is Second-Best Specialty Champion, it receives 90 percent of the points received by the Best Specialty Champion.

If your cat is called up for Finals as Best *Champion*, but does not receive a rosette, it receives 1 Grand Championship point for *every* benched Champion it defeated. If it is Second-Best Champion, it receives 90 percent of the points received by the Best Champion.

If your cat makes the Finals and is the highest-ranking Champion, it receives 1 Grand Championship point for each benched *Champion* it defeated. This is *not* the same as being Best Cat. You might have the Second-Best Cat, but the highest-ranking Champion, since the cat that finished above your cat is a Grand Champion. From there, you count from the Champion that placed second-highest in the Finals. It receives 90 percent of the points received by the highest-placing Champion. The third receives 80 percent, the fourth 70 percent, and so on until the tenth-highest, which receives 10 percent.

When tabulating points, there are a few basic rules to keep in mind. First, fractional points from .5 and above are rounded to the next higher number. Second, in all cases, your cat can get points from only *one* award per ring—the one that carries the most points. And third, your cat must have at least one win of Best Champion or Second-Best Champion or a Final award from Best to Tenth-Best Cat in order to qualify for the title Grand Champion. That means your cat cannot become a Grand Champion by accumulating points at the breed and division level only.

Once your cat has received enough points to become a Grand Champion, you *must* enter it in future shows as a Grand Champion. CFA's central office will keep track of the points you earn toward your Grand Championship. It will automatically confirm your cat as a Grand Champion. If you are not sure about the cat's status, call the CFA office *before* your next show to find out if it has completed the requirements for a Grand Championship

PREMIERS

In CFA, altered cats are called Premiers, a name taken from the title for which they compete, Premiership. Premiers are judged and scored in the same way as Championship cats, except that the titles they compete for are the Premiership (like Championship) and the Grand Premiership (like Grand Championship), and the cats they are seeking to defeat are other Premiers. An Alter that has won six winner's ribbons from at least four different judges is awarded the title of Premiership. However, to become a Grand Premier, it must collect 75 Grand Premiership points (not 150, like a Champion) under at least three different judges.

HOUSEHOLD PET CATS AND KITTENS

In CFA, Household Pet kittens and adults are judged together. They are judged solely on the basis of their beauty and condition and are awarded a Merit ribbon in recognition of their general condition and presentation. From there, they compete for Finals only. CFA does not award titles to Household Pet cats.

Longhair and shorthair Household Pets are judged together, as are kittens (four to eight months old) and adults (eight or more months in age). The judges award Finals for the Best through the Tenth-Best Household Pet Cat.

Colors of Flats
  Class
      First Place   Dark Blue
      Second Place   Red
      Third Place   Yellow
    Winner   Red, White and Blue
    Merit   Red and White
  Color
    Best   Black
    Second-Best   White
  Division
    Best   Brown
    Second-Best   Gold
  Breed
    Best   Brown
    Second-Best   Gold
  Champion
    Best   Purple
    Second-Best   *

*No color specified. Typically, it is a color other than one used for another flat.

214

APPENDIX III

Keeping Score in CFF

PUREBRED KITTENS

Kittens do not compete for titles in CFF. The first step for judging a kitten is for it to be judged against other kittens in a "color class," that is, kittens of the same color, in the same breed, and of the same sex. The judge will award first through third place to each kitten in the color class. Then the judge looks at all of the color classes making up a breed and awards a Best of Breed and Second-Best of Breed.

The judge then reviews all of the shorthair or longhair kittens and awards rosettes in Finals to the top ten kittens. If the judge is "All-Breed," the top ten cover both longhair and shorthair kittens.

CHAMPIONSHIP CATS

The first step for judging a cat in CFF is for it to be judged in the "novice" class—that is, with cats that have not yet become Champions. Each cat is placed in a color class and judged with other novices. The judge will award first through third place to each novice in the color class. Then, the best male novice and the best female novice of each color class will be awarded a winner's ribbon.

A novice that has won four winner's ribbons from at least three different judges is awarded the title of Champion.

The judge also judges *all* of the cats in the color class, including novices, Champions, Grand Champions and Master Grand Champions. In that judging, the judge awards a Best and Second-Best of Color Class. Then the judge looks at all of the color classes making up a breed and awards a Best of Breed and Second-Best of Breed.

Then the judge reviews all of the shorthair or longhair cats and awards rosettes in Finals to the top ten cats. If the judge is "All-Breed," the top ten cover both longhair and shorthair adult cats.

That means that a cat shown as a novice might win a first and a winner's ribbon, but only receive a Second-Best of Color Class if another cat of the same color that is already a Champion defeats it.

Each judge also announces the top Champions in Show in that ring. These may or may not be among the top ten Finalists. Also, the judge announces his or her Best and Second-Best Grand Champion, which also may or may not be among the top ten Finalists. The determination of the Best Champion and Best Grand Champion is used to determine what additional titles are awarded.

In CFF, after Champion, an adult cat can become a Grand Champion and then a Master Grand Champion.

To become a Grand Champion, first the cat must already be a Champion. Then it must earn 150 points, and earn them under at least three different judges. It earns points this way: If it is Best Champion in Show, it gets one point for each similar Champion it defeats. So, in a Specialty ring, such as shorthair, a Siamese Champion that is Best Shorthair Champion would get one point for every Champion it defeated. If the ring is All-Breed, it gets a point for each Shorthair (but *not* Longhair) Champion it defeats. In CFF, a cat is considered to have defeated every cat that is announced as "benched" at the show. That means if a Champion cat is present in the showhall for judging, but is not brought to a particular ring, and your cat is the Best Champion, you still get a point for defeating that cat.

The Second-Best Champion gets one point less than the Best Champion. The Best and Second-Best Champions earn these points even if they do not make the Finals.

A cat which is the Third-Best through the Fifth-Best Champion can also collect points, but it has to make the Finals. If it makes the Finals, the Third-Best Champion get 75 percent of the points given to the Second-Best Champion. The Fourth-Best Champion, if it makes the Finals, gets 50 percent of the points given the Second-Best Champion. The Fifth-Best Champion, again, only if it makes the Finals, gets 25 percent of the number of points given to the Second-Best Champion.

In addition to the 150 points, to become a CFF Grand Champion, the CFF Champion must also have finished among the top five cats at least once as a Champion. It does not matter whether the top five rosette was in an All-Breed or Specialty ring.

The last title in the series is that of Master Grand Champion. First, your cat must have been confirmed as a Grand Champion in CFF. Then, it must have earned an additional 100 points in CFF shows as a Grand Champion. These points must have been earned under at least six different judges. These points are awarded as follows: If your cat is judged as the Best Grand Champion, in either an All-Breed or Specialty ring, it earns 1 point for each benched Grand Champion competing.

If your cat is judged the Second-Best Grand Champion, it earns one point less than the Best Grand Champion earned.

In addition, as a Grand Champion, your cat must have been judged the Best Cat in at least one ring, All-Breed or Specialty.

ALTERS

Alters are judged and scored in the same way as Championship cats, except that the titles they compete for add the word Altered, to make them Altered Champion, Altered Grand Champion and Altered Master Grand Champion. The cats they are seeking to defeat are other Altered Champions. An Alter that has won four winner's ribbons from at least three different judges is awarded the title of Altered Champion. However, to become an Altered Grand Champion, it must collect 80 (not 150, like a Champion) points under at least three different judges. To become an Altered Master Grand Champion, it must collect 75 (not 100, like a Champion) points under at least six different judges.

HOUSEHOLD PET CATS AND KITTENS

In CFF, all Household Pets, regardless of age, as long as they are at least four months old, are judged together as Household Pet cats.

CFF does not require that Household Pet cats be altered in order to be shown. However, an individual club may require that these cats be altered in order to be shown. If the club requires that, it must let you know in its show flyer.

Household Pet cats are judged only as All-Breed, and not as either shorthair or longhair. The first step for judging a Household Pet cat or kitten is for it to be judged against other Household Pets placed in the same "color class"—that is, it is judged with cats or kittens of the same color and of the same sex.

Then the judge selects his or her Best from among all of the Household Pet cats and kittens. If there are fifteen or fewer entries, the judge will announce the Best through the Fifth-Best Household Pet. If there are sixteen or more entries, the judge will announce the top ten Household Pets.

To receive the title of Companion, your Household Pet must receive one Final in an All-Breed ring. The next title is that of Grand Companion. For this, your Household Pet cat or kitten must already be confirmed as a Companion, and must then receive five top ten All-Breed Finals under three different judges.

The highest title is that of Master Grand Companion. To earn that, your Household Pet cat must first have been confirmed as a Grand Companion. Then it must receive at least six Finals under three different judges. One of those must be a Best Cat Final.

Colors of Flats
Class
    First Place   Dark Blue
    Second Place Red
    Third Place   Yellow
Winner   Purple
Merit   *
Color
    Best   White
    Second-Best   Light Blue
Breed
    Best   Black
    Second-Best   Gold
Champion
    Best   *
    Second-Best   *

*No color specified. Typically, it is a color other than one in use for another flat.

APPENDIX IV

Keeping Score in TICA

PUREBRED KITTENS

The first step in judging in TICA is the "color" ribbon, which is awarded for a cat's achieving Standard, not really on color alone. All kittens of the same color and pattern in each breed compete for the ribbon. The winner receives a Best of Color and so on down to Fifth-Best.

A judge then compares all those kittens within the same division of a breed (for example, solid and white). The judge awards a Best of Division, a Second-Best and a Third-Best. Kittens are not formally judged as Best of Breed, Second-Best of Breed or Third-Best of Breed. However, many judges will announce the Best, Second-Best and Third-Best of Breed in the kitten ring.

The judge then decides on the top ten kittens in that ring, whether longhair, shorthair or all kittens. The judge presents rosettes, numbered one through ten. Kittens do not compete for Championship titles.

TICA requires that a judge present (or "hang") ten rosettes if there are twenty-five or more kittens (or cats, Alters, HHP kittens, or HHPs) competing. Otherwise, the judge need only present the top five rosettes. However, many judges will present all ten rosettes, if the club has made them available.

Kittens in TICA compete each year for regional and national awards. Here, the points that count are *only* those for Finals, plus a bonus awarded for kittens defeated.

CHAMPIONSHIP CATS

The first step in TICA judging is the "color" ribbon, which is awarded for a cat's achieving Standard, not really on color alone. All cats of the same color and pattern in each breed compete for the ribbon, whether they are novices or Supreme Grand Champions.

The winner receives a Best of Color, worth 25 points. A Second-Best of Color is worth 20, a Third-Best 15 and so on down to Fifth-Best.

The judge then compares all those cats within the same division of a breed (for example, tabby). The judge awards a Best of Division (25), a Second-Best (20) and a Third-Best (15).

Next, all those in the same breed are judged against one another, and Best, Second-Best and Third-Best of Breed are presented. These carry *no* points.

The judge then decides on the top ten cats in that ring, whether it is longhair, shorthair or all cats. The judge presents rosettes, numbered one through ten. The point value of the rosettes depends on two factors: how many cats were judged in total, and whether the ring is All-Breed or Specialty.

If twenty-five or more cats were judged, all of the rosettes carry points, and for that reason are often called "point Finals." If twenty-four or fewer were judged, then only the top five carry points. All-Breed rosettes start at 200 points for Best, and decrease by tens to 110 for Tenth-Best. Specialty rosettes start at 150 points and also decrease by tens to 60 points for Tenth-Best.

In addition, cats are awarded points for the number of cats defeated, whether or not the rosette carries points.

How Are the Points Used?

For a novice to become a Champion, it must get at least 300 points from color, division and Finals. These must come from at least four different judges. It must also receive a rosette that carries some points.

To go from Champion to Grand Champion, a cat must have a total of 1,000 points from color, division and Finals. It must also receive at least five *more* Finals from four different judges. All of these Finals must be point Finals and three of the six must be from any combination of the top five Specialty or top ten All-Breed.

Once your cat is a Grand Champion, to move to Double Grand Champion, it must have 2,000 points and one point Final *as* a Grand Champion. To move from Double Grand to Triple Grand Champion requires 3,000 points and an *additional* point Final. To move to Quadruple Grand Champion, your cat must amass 4,000 points and one *more* point Final *as* a Triple Champion.

The last step is Supreme Grand Champion. To receive this title, your cat must amass 6,000 points, and, *after* it is a Quadruple Grand Champion, it must receive one Best Cat rosette, in either an All-Breed or a Specialty ring.

ALTERS

In TICA, Alters also compete for the title Champion. The way in which Alters are judged and scored is identical with that used for Championship cats.

HOUSEHOLD PET KITTENS

The first step in judging in TICA is the "Merit" ribbon, which is awarded based on an examination of the kitten's overall condition and well-being. Then a judge compares all those kittens within the same division (for example, solid). The judge awards a Best of Division, a Second-Best and a Third-Best.

There is no breed judging of Household Pet kittens, since there are no breeds.

The judge then decides on the top ten kittens in that ring, whether longhair, shorthair or all kittens. The judge presents rosettes, numbered one through ten. HHP kittens do not compete for titles.

HOUSEHOLD PET CATS

The first step in judging in TICA is the "Merit" ribbon, which is awarded based on an examination of the cat's overall condition and well-being. A Household Pet cat receiving a Merit ribbon also receives 25 points.

The judge then compares all those cats within the same division (for example, pointed). The judge awards a Best of Division (25), a Second-Best (20) and a Third-Best (15). There is no breed judging in Household Pets, since there are no breeds.

The judge then decides on the top ten cats, whether longhair, shorthair or all cats. The judge presents rosettes, numbered one through ten. The point value of the rosettes depends on two factors: how many cats were judged in total, and whether the ring is All-Breed or Specialty.

If twenty-five or more cats were judged, all of the rosettes carry points, and for that reason are often called "point Finals." If twenty-four or fewer were judged, only the top five carry points.

All-Breed rosettes start at 200 points for Best, and decrease by tens to 110 for Tenth-Best. Specialty rosettes start at 150 points and also decrease by tens to 60 points for Tenth-Best.

In addition, cats are awarded points for the number of cats defeated, regardless of whether the rosette carries points with it.

How Are the Points Used?

All HHPs start as "seniors"—that is, cats without any title. For a senior to become a Master, the first step, it must get at least 300 points from merit, division and Finals. Also, it must receive a rosette that carries with it some points.

To go from Master to Grand Master, it must first become a Champion. Then it must have a total of 1,000 points from color, division and Finals. It must also receive at least five *more* Finals from four different judges. All of these Finals must be point Finals and three of the six must be from any combination of the top five Specialty or top ten All-Breed.

Once your cat is a Grand Master, to move to Double Grand Master, it must have 2,000 points and one point Final *as* a Grand Champion. To move from Double Grand to Triple Grand Master requires 3,000 points and an *additional* point Final. For Quadruple Grand Master, your cat must amass 4,000 points and one more point Final *as* a Triple Master.

The last step is Supreme Grand Master. To receive this title, your cat must amass 6,000 points, and *after* it is a Quadruple Grand Master, it must receive one Best Cat rosette, either in All-Breed *or* Specialty.

Colors of Flats
  Merit   *
  Color
    Best   Dark Blue
    Second-Best   Red
    Third-Best   Yellow
    Fourth-Best   Green
    Fifth-Best   White
  Division
    Best   Black

Second-Best	Purple
Third-Best	Orange
Breed	
Best	†
Second-Best	†
Third-Best	†

*No color specified. Typically, it is a color other than one in use for another ribbon or flat.
†The rules state that there is no specific ribbon for this award. However, most clubs provide the judges with a flat designating the finishes (placings) within each breed.